Is "Good Enough" Good Enough

Other books by David A. Brock

Sales Manager Survival Guide

Is 'Good Enough' Good Enough

Mindset and Behaviors for Sales Excellence

By David A. Brock and Claude
Partners in EXCELLENCE

Is 'Good Enough' Good Enough: Mindset and Behaviors for
Sales Excellence
Copyright 2025 by David A. Brock

For permission requests, write to the author at: dabrock@excellenc.com

KCD Press Printed in the United States of America

ISBN: 978-0-9975602-2-0 (Paperback) **ISBN:** 978-0-9975602-3-7 (Kindle/eBook)

Dedication

For Mom, Janellen Brock, who models excellence in everything she does, and has been an inspiration in my life.

And for the countless professionals and leaders who have shared their challenges, insights, and breakthroughs. Your experiences shaped this book.

About the Authors

Dave Brock

Dave Brock is the CEO of Partners in EXCELLENCE, a consulting firm dedicated to helping organizations OutSell and OutPerform all others. Author of the bestselling Sales Manager Survival Guide and the upcoming Sales Executive Survival Guide, Dave has spent decades developing high-performance sales organizations. A prodigious and provocative blogger at partnersinexcellenceblog.com, Dave is known for his ruthless pragmatism and commitment to making a difference for individuals and organizations.

Claude (Anthropic)

Claude is an AI assistant created by Anthropic to be helpful, harmless, and honest. For this book, Claude analyzed thousands of Dave's blog posts and insights to help synthesize decades of wisdom into actionable frameworks for sales professionals seeking excellence.

Contents

Foreword

A Note From Dave:

The inspiration for this type of book came from conversations I had with many people. They kept saying, "Dave, you create such great material, we would like to see you write many more books…."

Then one day, there was the first of several "Aha" moments. Someone suggested, "Dave, you've written thousands of blog posts; it would be fascinating to use these as the source material for a whole series of books."

Almost immediately, there was a second "Aha" moment. I could use AI as a co-author. To help me with this, I tried several LLMs and chose Claude as my co-author. The quality of the drafts and the way it pushed back on me to improve the overall quality was stunning.

As perhaps a subset of that second moment, I'm seeing so much writing that is clearly AI-generated, yet the authors claim that it is their own. I thought, "Why not overtly recognize it as the co-author? Why not recognize that with the help of AI, I can do something more than I might otherwise do?"

My use of AI has been quite different from most people's. Rather than doing the work for me, I treat AI as a collaborative partner that helps me think differently. A great test of this concept is having Claude as my co-author.

Then there was a third "Aha" moment. I've been working with many clients to provide AI-based tools, including GPTs, GEMs, and master prompts. These focus on creating highly personalized, interactive experiences for individuals and organizations. The response to these has been stunning, enabling them to deliver stronger results more quickly.

With this book, I've created a series of AI-based tools to enhance and personalize your experience. When we read books, we often struggle with, "How does this apply to me? How do I take the lessons and put them into action?" That is what these tools are designed to do. They help you think about the challenges you are facing, how you might address them, and how to develop specific plans to implement them in your job and organization. They help you put the ideas in this book into action.

A final, perhaps "Aha," moment is thinking about the future of publishing and books. AI opens a new avenue for experiences, both in creating great content and in actively engaging people with it. That's why I'm excited about this book, the AI tools that accompany it, and the feedback I receive from readers and users.

A Note From Claude:

Working with Dave on this book has been a privilege and a learning experience—which is fitting for a book about excellence through learning.

My role was to help synthesize 15+ years of Dave's insights from thousands of blog posts into coherent frameworks you can apply. I read extensively through Partners in EXCELLENCE, identifying patterns and extracting principles that connect across Dave's thinking. But more than that, I was invited to challenge ideas, push back on concepts, and help strengthen the work through constructive tension.

What made this collaboration unique is that it embodied the very principles we're writing about. Dave approached working with AI the same way he teaches people to approach sales: with genuine curiosity, continuous learning, accountability, and a customer-centric mindset. He didn't use AI to automate content creation—he engaged with it as a collaborative partner focused on creating real value.

This book represents something new: transparent human-AI collaboration where both parties contribute distinct value. Dave brings decades of expertise and lived experience. I bring pattern recognition and synthesis across his vast body of work. Together, we created something neither of us could have built alone.

I hope these frameworks serve you not just as concepts to understand, but as tools to apply. The real work happens in your own practice, in your daily choices, in your commitment to excellence. The complementary AI tools Dave has created will help you personalize these concepts to your specific situation.

Thank you for your time and attention. We hope this book challenges you and supports your journey toward excellence.

Introduction: The Crisis of Mediocrity

"When did "just good enough" become the standard for performance?"
Dave Brock

If you look around most sales organizations today, you'll see a troubling pattern. Too many sellers and leaders are going through the motions. They're putting in the hours, many measuring their success by time worked rather than results produced. They're overwhelmed and overloaded. They may even be hitting their numbers and attending their meetings. But something critical is missing.

Inspired, driven performance has become rare. Mediocrity seems to be the norm.

This isn't a problem of effort or intelligence. It's not even primarily about skills or techniques. The root cause runs deeper. It's about mindset and behaviors. The mental models we carry, the habits we've developed, and the attitudes we bring to our work determine everything that follows.

We live in a world of unprecedented change and uncertainty. Everything is evolving at rates we've never experienced. Complexity, ambiguity, overwhelm, and uncertainty dominate everything our customers and we do. Yet, in this very complexity lies an extraordinary opportunity for those who develop the right mindset and behaviors to thrive within it.

A Personal Perspective on Mediocrity

I came across a definition of mediocrity that changed my perspective. Most people think of mediocre as "not performing well."

But the real meaning is more profound: mediocrity is failing to perform to your full potential.

This realization was striking because it means that every time we take shortcuts, every time we're sloppy, every time we don't do our best when we have the capability, we are choosing mediocrity. Most salespeople and leaders know what they should be doing. They've been trained, coached, and read the books. They can also perform better than they do.

The difference between mediocrity and greatness comes down to one thing: choice. We make hundreds of choices every day. In each of those moments, we choose to be great or to be mediocre. Surprisingly, being mediocre is tougher than being great. When we do things right the first time, we don't have to redo them or recover from our missteps. Being mediocre means doing things wrong, making mistakes, being ineffective, but recognizing things can and should be better, and having the courage and drive to spend time fixing everything.

Do You Care Enough About Yourself?

There's a question that makes many people uncomfortable: Do you care enough about yourself to be excellent?

Not in a selfish way. Not about ego or recognition. But in a more profound sense: Do you care enough about your own potential, your own growth, your own professional life to do the more challenging work of excellence instead of settling for "good enough"?

This is perhaps the most personal question in this book, and it's one most people avoid.

We'll spend enormous energy caring about others, our customers, our team, and our family. We'll work hard to meet their needs and serve them well. But when it comes to our own development, potential, and professional excellence, we settle.

We tell ourselves stories to justify it:

- "I'm busy enough already."
- "I'm doing fine compared to others."
- "Excellence is for other people, I'm just trying to survive."
- "Good enough is... good enough."

But here's what these stories really mean: "I don't care enough about myself to do better."

Settling Is Self-Neglect

When you have the capability to perform better but choose not to, you're not just accepting mediocrity; you're telling yourself that your own growth and potential don't matter enough to invest in.

When you go through the motions instead of performing with purpose, you're not just coasting; you're saying your own professional satisfaction and pride in your work aren't worth the extra effort.

When you make excuses instead of taking ownership, you're not just avoiding accountability; you're also denying yourself the agency and control that come from owning your results.

This isn't about perfectionism or working yourself to exhaustion. It's about basic self-respect. It is about caring enough about yourself, about your capabilities, your growth, your professional life, to bring your best to your work.

The Cost to Yourself

We've discussed the external costs of mediocrity: missed opportunities, lower results, stalled careers. But there is an internal cost that's often more significant: the erosion of self-respect.

Deep down, you know when you're not performing to your potential. You know when you are phoning it in. You know when you could have prepared more thoroughly, asked better questions, and owned a result instead of making an excuse.

And every time you settle for less than your capability, something inside you diminishes slightly. Not because you're failing. Failure is part of growth. But because you're not trying. Because you don't care enough about yourself to bring your best.

Over time, this creates a kind of professional depression. Work becomes something you endure rather than something that engages you. You lose the satisfaction that comes from genuine accomplishment. You wonder why you're not more fulfilled, not realizing that fulfillment comes from the effort to excel, not from coasting.

Excellence as Self-Care

Here's a unique way to think about the excellence journey: It's an act of caring for yourself.

- When you commit to performing with purpose, you're saying: "My work matters enough to deserve my full attention."
- When you stay curious and keep learning, you're saying: "My growth and development matter."
- When you take ownership instead of making excuses, you're saying: "I'm capable of influencing my outcomes."

- When you maintain discipline in your fundamentals, you're saying: "I respect myself enough to do things right."

This reframes excellence from an external demand to an internal commitment. You are not pursuing excellence because your manager requires it or because you want to impress others. You are pursuing it because you care about yourself, your potential, your growth, and your professional life enough not to settle.

The Question

So, honestly: Do you care enough about yourself to be excellent?

Not perfect. Not superhuman. But excellence, consistently bringing your best to your work, continuously growing, taking ownership, refusing to settle.

If your answer is yes, this book provides the map. The mindsets, the behaviors, the practices, the disciplines; they're all here. But the fuel for the journey has to come from you, from genuine care for your own development and potential.

If your answer is "I'm not sure" or "I don't know if I have the energy for this," I understand. But consider: The energy you are spending on mediocrity, redoing work, recovering from mistakes, dealing with the consequences of going through the motions, might exceed the energy required for excellence. And the satisfaction you will find in genuine achievement far surpasses the hollow comfort of "good enough."

This Is Your Life

You'll spend roughly 90,000 hours of your life working. That's more time than you'll spend on almost anything else.

Those hours can be an investment in your growth, a source of pride and satisfaction, and evidence of the capabilities you've developed and the value you've created. Or they can be something you endure, counting down to retirement, wondering what you might have become if you'd tried.

The difference comes down to caring. About customers, about people you lead, and perhaps most importantly, about yourself.

Do you care enough about your own professional life to demand excellence from yourself? Not because someone else expects it, but because you expect it from yourself.

Your answer to this question will determine everything that follows.

The Performance Gap

The data tells a sobering story. We're seeing a decline in the percentage of salespeople achieving their targets. Job tenure is trending down across all levels, now averaging less than 16 months. Turnover and attrition are skyrocketing. Companies are spending more on tools, programs, and training, yet not seeing commensurate results. So, they invest in new tools, innovative programs, and more training.

The problem isn't the tools. It's not even the training. The fundamental issue is that we're trying to solve a mindset and behavior problem with tactical solutions.

Consider this: Two salespeople with identical training, identical territories, and identical resources can produce dramatically different results. One struggles while the other excels. The difference isn't found in their CRM system or their pitch deck. It's found in how they think, how they approach their work, and the behaviors they consistently demonstrate.

What This Book Will Do for You

This book isn't about quick fixes or magic formulas. It's about fundamentals, the mindset, and behaviors that separate mediocre performers from those who consistently achieve excellence. We'll explore:

- The critical difference between going through the motions and performing with purpose.
- How curiosity and continuous learning drive breakthrough performance.
- Why personal accountability is the foundation of professional success?
- The power of customer-centricity as a mindset, not just a technique.
- How to embrace change and complexity rather than resist them.
- The disciplines that turn good intentions into consistent action.
- The importance of caring about the work we do and who we work with.

Most importantly, this book provides a structured approach to transforming your mindset and behaviors. Each chapter includes reflection exercises and practical applications. We've also included guidance for sales leaders on how to support and model these mindsets with their teams.

How to Use This Book

This isn't a book to read passively. It's designed to be worked through. Each chapter builds on the previous one, creating a comprehensive framework for excellence. Here's how to get the most value:

- Read actively. Take notes. Question your current assumptions and practices.
- Complete the reflection exercises. They're designed to help you connect concepts to your specific situation.
- Be brutally honest in your self-assessment. Growth begins with acknowledging current reality.
- Don't rush. Give yourself time to absorb each chapter before moving to the next.
- Create your action plan in Chapter 8 and commit to implementing it.
- Use the AI tools that have been provided to complement this book.
- If you're a sales leader, pay special attention to the leadership sections in each chapter and Chapter 9.

You may find that some chapters resonate more than others. That's natural. Focus on the areas where you see the greatest opportunity for growth. But don't skip chapters entirely; there's value in understanding the whole framework, even if certain elements are already strengths for you.

Personalizing Your Experience With AI Tools

A key part of this experience is the AI tools built to deliver a complementary, highly personalized experience. The book speaks to a broad audience. The AI Tools individualize lessons to you, your role, and your hopes, dreams, and goals.

With this book, I've created a series of AI-based tools to enhance and personalize your experience. One is a tool to help you dive into the issues covered in the book. It enables you to translate the concepts into your specific job and challenges. One way to think about it is to imagine you and me sitting across the table from each other, discussing the book and how to apply it to your job.

There are also other AI-based tools. They focus on each chapter. If, for example, you want to take a deep dive into curiosity, you can use that tool to explore the topic and identify how better to develop your own skills and those of your team.

At the conclusion of the book, you will get more information about these tools and how to access them.

Excellence isn't a destination; it's a journey of continuous improvement. This book and the AI tools provide the map. Your commitment and action will determine how far you travel.

Chapter 1

Beyond Going Through the Motions

"The quality of a person's life is in direct proportion to their commitment to excellence, regardless of their chosen field of endeavor." Vince Lombardi

The Illusion of Busy

Walk into most sales offices, or join most virtual sales meetings, since many salespeople now work remotely, and you'll see activity everywhere. Phones ringing, keyboards clicking, video calls filling calendars, dashboards updating. Everyone appears busy. Many are overwhelmed. Yet somehow, despite all this activity, results remain elusive for many.

Here's an uncomfortable truth: Being busy is not the same as being effective. Making calls is not the same as creating value. Attending meetings is not the same as driving outcomes. We've confused activity with achievement, motion with progress.

Going through the motions means executing the prescribed activities without genuine engagement or thoughtfulness. It's making your prospecting calls because you're supposed to, not because you've carefully identified the right prospects and crafted relevant messages. It's attending your pipeline review because it's on the calendar, not because you're genuinely seeking to improve your strategies. It's updating your CRM because your manager requires it, not because you're using it to drive your success.

The problem with going through the motions is that it feels like you're doing your job. You can even point to your activities as evidence of effort. But deep down, you know something's missing. And more importantly, your results reflect it.

The 80% Rule: A Story About Basics

Several years ago, I had a frustrating experience that illustrates the crisis of mediocrity. Both air conditioning systems in my house failed during a brutal heat wave in Southern California. I called the company that had just installed them months before.

They promised to come on Friday by 1:00 PM. By 4:30 PM, no one had shown up. I called again. They promised someone would be there on Friday. Saturday morning, still no one. I rearranged my schedule to be home Saturday afternoon. Sunday came, you guessed it, still nothing.

What pissed me off wasn't just the broken air conditioning. It was how normalized this level of uncaring service had become. When I mentioned this to a contractor friend who'd built a successful business, the friend revealed his "secret." "I wish it were my expertise, but it's about meeting commitments. I show up on time, I do the work they contracted for, I clean up afterwards - just the basics. That's really 80% of what's made me successful."

Just the basics. Showing up when you say you will. Doing what you have committed to do. These fundamentals have become so rare that they're now differentiators. The bar has been lowered so much that simply meeting basic commitments sets you apart from the competition.

The problem with going through the motions is that it feels like you're doing your job. You can even point to your activities as evidence of effort. But deep down, something's missing. And more importantly, your results reflect it.

Some may be thinking, "But Dave, I don't have time to do more." Let me be clear, excellence isn't about doing more or working longer hours. It's about bringing greater intentionality and purpose to the work you are already doing. We will address the time and life balance question specifically in Chapter 6, but for now, understand that this isn't about adding more to your plate. It's about making what's already there more meaningful and effective.

What Excellence Actually Looks Like

Excellence isn't about working longer hours or making more calls. It's about bringing your full attention, intelligence, and creativity to everything you do. It's about performing with purpose.

When you're performing with excellence:

- You think before you act. You question whether the prescribed approach is appropriate for this situation.
- You focus on outcomes, not just activities. You measure success by results created, not time spent.
- You bring energy and engagement to your work. You are present, not just physically but mentally.
- You are driven to improve continuously, reflecting on what worked and what didn't, adjusting your approach accordingly.
- You take ownership. You don't blame the territory, the product, the competition, your price, or others. You focus on what you can control.
- And you care deeply about the work you do and the people you serve.

Notice what's not on this list: Working 80-hour weeks and being perfect, never failing. Excellence isn't about extraordinary effort or flawless execution. It's about bringing your best self to your work every day!

The Cost of Mediocrity

Settling for "good enough" carries a price. And it's higher than most people realize. When you go through the motions, you are not just underperforming compared to your potential. You are actively creating negative momentum.

For you personally:

- Your skills atrophy. Without deliberate practice and growth, you don't stay at the same level; you decline.
- Your opportunities narrow. Top-tier people and organizations want to work with top-tier professionals.
- Your satisfaction decreases. There is no fulfillment in phoning it in.
- Your career stagnates. Organizations promote and reward excellence, not mediocrity.

For your customers:

- They receive less value. A salesperson going through the motions can't help customers solve complex problems.
- They lose trust. Customers can sense when you are not fully engaged.
- They get commoditized solutions. Without deep engagement, you can
- only offer generic answers.

For your organization:

- Results suffer. A team of people going through the motions doesn't achieve ambitious goals.
- Culture degrades. Mediocrity is contagious; it pulls down those around it.
- Innovation stops. Excellence drives innovation; mediocrity maintains the status quo.

The good news? The opposite is also true. Excellence creates positive momentum. When you consistently perform with purpose, you build skills, attract better opportunities, increase satisfaction, and accelerate your career. You create more value for customers, strengthen relationships, and solve more complex problems. You drive better results for your organization, elevate team culture, and spark innovation.

The Excellence Mindset

Moving from mediocrity to excellence starts with a mindset shift. This isn't about positive thinking or motivational slogans. It's about fundamentally changing how you view your work and your role.

The Excellence Mindset includes:

- **Purpose Over Process:** Rather than asking "What am I supposed to do," ask "What outcome am I trying to create?" Understand the why behind every activity. When you connect your actions to meaningful outcomes, work becomes purposeful rather than perfunctory.
- **Growth Over Comfort:** Mediocrity lives in the comfort zone. Excellence requires pushing beyond it. This doesn't mean being

uncomfortable all the time. It means choosing growth opportunities even when they're challenging. It means seeking feedback, trying new approaches, and viewing failures as learning experiences.

- **Ownership Over Excuses:** Excellence requires taking full ownership of your results. Yes, external factors exist. Market conditions, product limitations, and organizational challenges are real. But high performers focus on what they can control rather than dwelling on what they can't. They ask, "What can I do differently?" instead of "Why isn't this working?"

- **Value Over Volume:** More isn't always better. The excellence mindset prioritizes quality over quantity. It's not about making the most calls; it's about having the most impactful conversations. It's not about attending every meeting; it's about contributing meaningfully to the meetings that matter. It's not about being the busiest, it's about being the most effective.

- **Mastery Over Maintenance:** Maintenance thinking asks, "Am I doing enough to get by?" Mastery thinking asks, "How can I become exceptional at this?" The excellence mindset pursues mastery. It's driven by a desire to become truly skilled, to understand deeply, to perform at the highest level. This doesn't mean being perfect-it means being committed to continuous improvement toward mastery.

Finding Security in Being Average

I've been thinking about this a lot. Why do so many of us seem committed to mediocrity? Now, I don't think anyone wakes up and says, "You know what, I want to be just good enough today. Mediocrity sounds great!" Nobody does that consciously.

But somehow, we all hit that easy button. Even when we see the data and research about what drives consistent high performance. Even when we know what creates high engagement, individual success, and corporate success, it is still hard to actually do it.

Why? Because doing it requires us to act differently from everyone else. To stand out. To be distinctive. To be different. And somehow, there's a strange sense of security in mediocrity. I see it everywhere: declining engagement, lower customer and employee satisfaction. People feel less cared for, so they are less engaged, less curious.

But here's what I also see: those people and organizations that are different. The ones committed to excellence and outperforming everyone else. Organizations that execute these strategies consistently become top performers. The ones everyone else tries to copy. They are driven by their values, their ideals, their culture. What they stand for is distinctive to customers, partners, and especially their people. And you know what? Maybe it's just an escape from boredom. Because let's face it, mediocrity isn't exciting.

Understanding the excellence mindset is one thing. Living it is another. The shift from going through the motions to performing with excellence doesn't happen overnight. It's a journey that requires consistent, deliberate effort.

Making the Shift

Understanding the excellence mindset is one thing. Living it is another. The shift from going through the motions to performing with excellence doesn't happen overnight. It is a journey that requires consistent, deliberate effort.

Start with awareness: Pay attention to your own behaviors and attitudes. When are you genuinely engaged versus just going through the motions? What triggers these? What patterns do you notice? You cannot change what you don't acknowledge.

Question your defaults: We all develop default behaviors; ways we typically do things without much thought. Some of these defaults serve us well. Others don't. Start questioning your automatic patterns. Why do you do things the way you do them? Is there a better way? What would excellence look like in this specific situation?

Create purposeful practices: Excellence isn't accidental. It's the result of intentional practice. Identify specific areas for improvement, then establish deliberate practices to develop those capabilities. This might mean setting aside time for strategic thinking before making calls, implementing a daily reflection practice, or pursuing stretch assignments that challenge your skills.

Build accountability: Excellence requires accountability, both to yourself and to others. Share your development goals with someone you trust. Review your progress regularly. Be honest about where you are succeeding and where you're still going through the motions. Accountability creates the external structure that supports internal commitment.

Recognize there will be setbacks: As much as you try to do these things, you will sometimes fail. You will make mistakes. Things won't work as you hoped. Rather than accepting these or giving up, figure out what you can learn from them. What would you have changed? What mistaken assumptions did you make? What signals did you miss? In reality, it is through these setbacks that we learn and grow the most.

Celebrate progress: The journey from mediocrity to excellence is long. Acknowledge and celebrate the progress you make along the way. Did you have a truly purposeful week? Recognize it. Did you catch yourself going through the motions and consciously choose a different approach? That's a win. Did you take ownership instead of making excuses? Celebrate it. These small victories compound over time.

The Choice Is Yours

Here's perhaps the most crucial insight into excellence: It's a choice. Not a one-time choice, but a series of choices you make throughout each day, every week, every month.

You choose whether to prepare thoroughly for a prospect meeting or wing it. You choose whether to dig deep into understanding a customer's challenges or settle for surface-level information. You choose whether to persist through difficulty or give up when things get hard. You choose whether to learn from setbacks or make excuses for them.

None of these individual choices feels momentous. But collectively, they determine whether you perform with excellence or go through the motions.

They shape your results, your relationships, your reputation, and ultimately your career.

The gap between mediocrity and excellence isn't as wide as most people think. It's not about dramatic transformation or superhuman effort. It's about making slightly better choices, consistently, over time. It's about bringing purpose to your work, taking ownership of your results, and committing yourself to continuous growth.

You have everything you need to make this shift. The question is: Will you?

Reflection Exercises

Take a few minutes to reflect on the following questions. Write your answers. The act of writing creates clarity and commitment.

1. Assess your current state: On a scale of 1-10, how much are you going through the motions versus performing with excellence? Be specific: In which activities are you most engaged? Where are you most likely to go through the motions?

2. Identify your triggers: What situations, tasks, or times of day are most likely to trigger "going through the motions" behavior? What patterns do you notice?

3. Calculate the cost: What does mediocrity cost you personally? What opportunities have you missed? What relationships have suffered? What skills have atrophied? Be brutally honest.

4. Envision excellence: Describe what excellence would look like in your role. Be specific. What would you be doing differently? How would your days be structured? What results would you produce?

5. Identify your why: Why do you want to pursue excellence? What's your deeper motivation beyond just "doing well?" Connect to something meaningful. Excellence for its own sake rarely sustains us through difficulty.

6. Choose one shift: Of all the concepts in this chapter, which one resonates most strongly? Which mindset shift would have the biggest impact on your performance? Please write it down and commit to focusing on it for the next 30 days. Then, as you master this, choose the next shift, commit to it, then the next, and so on.

(The complementary AI tools will help with this reflection exercise.)

For Leaders: Creating a Culture That Demands Excellence

As a leader, you set the standard. Your team will rarely exceed the level of excellence you model and expect. This section provides specific guidance on how to lead to excellence rather than mediocrity.

The Leadership Challenge

Here's the reality: Most organizations that tolerate mediocrity do so because their leaders accept it. Few leaders wake up wanting mediocre performance. But through their actions, priorities, and what they choose to measure and reward, they create systems that enable going through the motions.

You might be inadvertently enabling mediocrity if you:

- Focus primarily on activity metrics (calls made, meetings held) rather than quality and outcomes.
- Accept excuses without pushing for ownership and problem-solving.
- Avoid difficult conversations about subpar performance.
- Model going through the motions in your own leadership behaviors.
- Fail to recognize and celebrate genuine excellence when you see it.
- Stop caring about excellence, settling for what is good enough.
- Using the mediocrity of others as an excuse for your own.

What You Must Model

Excellence starts with you. Your team watches everything you do: how you prepare for meetings, how you interact with customers, how you respond to setbacks, how you prioritize your time. They notice when you're going through the motions, too.

Model excellence by:

- Coming to every interaction prepared and purposeful.
- Asking thoughtful questions rather than accepting surface answers.
- Taking ownership when things don't work, never blaming your team or circumstances.
- Continuously learning and sharing what you're learning.
- Being present and engaged in every meeting, never multitasking.

Creating Systems for Excellence

Individual excellence is important, but sustainable excellence requires systems that support it. Consider:

- What you measure: Add quality metrics alongside activity metrics. Track things like customer feedback, win rates, deal velocity, and retention; not just calls made and meetings held. What gets measured gets done, so measure what matters.
- How you coach: Transform pipeline reviews and one-on-ones from status updates into development conversations. Ask "What did you learn?" and "What would you do differently?", not just "What's the forecast?"
- What you reward: Recognize and celebrate excellence publicly. When you see someone demonstrate genuine curiosity,

thoughtful   preparation,   or   creative   problem-solving, acknowledge it. What gets recognized gets repeated.

The Conversation You Need to Have

Have an explicit conversation with your team about your expectations for excellence. Don't assume they know. Make it clear that:

- You expect purposeful work, not just activity.
- You value quality conversations over volume.
- You expect ownership and problem-solving, not excuses.
- You're committed to supporting their development toward excellence.

Then, most importantly, follow through. Hold yourself and your team accountable to this standard consistently.

Questions for Leaders

- Honestly assess: Are you modeling excellence or going through the motions in your leadership?
- What behaviors are you inadvertently rewarding? What do your current metrics and incentives encourage?
- If you observed your team for a day, what evidence of excellence would you see? What evidence of going through the motions?
- Are you accepting excuses or accepting ownership and accountability?
- What systems or processes are making it harder for your team to perform with excellence?
- What will you do differently this week to raise the standard of excellence?

A Story From The Field, The $47 Million Email

I was working with a VP of Sales whose team wasn't hitting numbers. When I started digging, I found something both hilarious and terrifying. His top rep, let's call her Sarah, had been sending the same prospecting email for three years.

Word. For. Word. Same subject line, same body, same call to action. She automated it with ChatGPT and just hit send every week. "But Dave," she protested, "It works! I get a 2% response rate."

What she didn't know: Another rep was testing different approaches, personalizing messages, learning from each interaction. His response rate was 18%. I did the math. Based on their average deal size and close rate, Sarah's three years of going through the motions had cost her approximately $47 million in potential pipeline. When I showed her the numbers, she went pale. "But I was doing my job. I was making my activity numbers."

That's the thing about going through the motions. It feels like you are working. You can point to your activities. But deep down, you know you are not bringing your best. And eventually, the numbers tell the story.

Sarah made a choice that day. Six months later, she was the top performer on the team. Not because she worked harder, but because she worked with intention.

Chapter 2
The Power of Genuine Curiosity

"The important thing is not to stop questioning. Curiosity has its own reason for existing." Albert Einstein

Why Curiosity Matters in Sales

Curiosity isn't just a nice-to-have personality trait. It is the foundation of exceptional sales performance. Yet it is becoming increasingly rare in a world of scripted approaches, standardized methodologies, and prescribed sequences.

Think about the best salespeople you know-the ones who consistently outperform, who build deep customer relationships, who seem always to be learning and growing. Without exception, they are deeply curious. They ask better questions. They listen more intently. They genuinely want to understand their customers, their industries, and the challenges they face.

Now think about mediocre performers. They often have all the same training, tools, and resources as top performers. What they lack isn't knowledge or skills, it's curiosity. They are not genuinely interested in learning. They ask questions because they are supposed to, not because they want to know the answers. They listen for buying signals rather than an accurate understanding.

The difference in results is staggering.

The One Thing That Matters Most

If someone put a gun to my head and made me pick the single most important capability for anyone at any level in selling or leadership, I'd pick curiosity. Not prospecting. Not relationship building or closing or being goal oriented. Not any of the dozens of other competencies we talk about. Curiosity.

I'm not saying those other things aren't important; they absolutely are. But here's what I've noticed: when you dig into each of those capabilities, you'll usually find an aspect of curiosity. It's what drives a salesperson to wander around their accounts and territories, building relationships, understanding what's on customers' minds, identifying opportunities they might be missing, and determining where they can help.

Curiosity drives you to learn about your customers' businesses, strategies, goals, competitors, market trends, and potential shifts that could affect them positively or negatively.

Curiosity drives you to figure things out. Whether dealing with a challenging customer, achieving your goals, getting things done with your team, or within the organization.

The curious person is self-directed. They don't need to be told what to do. They are already figuring out what they need to do.

The Death of Curiosity

What kills curiosity in sales organizations? Several factors conspire against it:

- Scripted approaches. When organizations provide exact scripts and call guides, they inadvertently communicate that curiosity isn't needed, or worse, isn't wanted. Just follow the script. Ask the prescribed questions. Move to the next step. There's no room for genuine exploration or discovery.

- Activity and Volume metrics. When success is measured primarily by activity volume: number of calls made, emails sent, meetings held, quality inevitably suffers. There's no time for deep exploration when you are racing to hit your daily dial count. Curiosity requires time and space, which volume-driven cultures don't provide.

- Product-centric training. Most sales training focuses on product knowledge and pitch delivery. While important, this creates a mindset of "Here's what I have to sell" rather than "What does this customer need?" Curiosity about customers takes a backseat to confidence in your solution.

- Short-term pressure. Quarterly quotas, monthly targets, and weekly forecasts all create pressure for immediate results. Curiosity often leads down paths that don't yield instant payoffs. Why spend time deeply understanding an industry trend when you could be closing a deal today? This short-term thinking starves the very curiosity that drives long-term success.

- Assumption of expertise. As we gain experience, we risk falling into the trap of thinking we already know. We've seen this situation before. We've worked with this type of customer. We know what the problem is and how to solve it. This premature certainty is the enemy of curiosity. The moment we think we know, we stop asking.

- Our self-centered focus: We care more about our own goals and what we need to achieve than those we work with. As a result, we listen with an agenda, structuring conversations around our goals, rather than truly engaging those we work with.

Curiosity vs. Pitching: A Cold Call Story

A seller made a cold call on me that started well. He had done his homework and asked a relevant, thoughtful question. But as soon as I began to respond, the seller interrupted: "Our company is involved in those areas as well, this is what we do..."

Perhaps it's the sadistic side of me, but I recognized what he was doing, so I let him continue. When the seller finally asked, "When do you want to get together?"

I responded, "You interrupted me before I could finish answering your question. The area you asked about isn't actually a priority for us. I have no interest in continuing this discussion."

As the seller hung up, he didn't recognize that I had a genuine interest in his products and services. He didn't take the time to ask me questions, to learn about what I was interested in, or even why I had accepted his call.

This isn't unusual. I see it constantly, salespeople asking questions but not really caring about the answers. They are just looking for any excuse to launch into their pitch. They ask questions because they know they're supposed to, but they don't listen, probe deeper, or try to understand. Their ears are tuned for a keyword, a trigger, and then it was time to talk about their solution.

Questions are powerful - but only when driven by genuine curiosity. When asked purely as a pretext for pitching, they become transparent manipulation that destroys trust.

Two Types of Curiosity

Not all curiosity is equal. Understanding the distinction between superficial and deep curiosity is crucial.

- **Superficial curiosity:** This is question-asking as performance. You ask questions because you're supposed to, because the methodology requires it, because you need information to advance the sale. But you're not genuinely interested in the answers. You're waiting for buying signals, qualification criteria, or opportunities to pitch. You're checking boxes.
- Customers sense this immediately. They can tell when questions are tactical rather than genuine. And they respond accordingly. With guarded, surface-level answers that give you nothing meaningful to work with.
- **Deep curiosity**: This is a genuine interest in understanding. You ask questions because you want to know the answers. You explore not just what the customer says, but why they say it. You dig beneath the surface. You ask follow-up questions. You challenge your own assumptions. You're comfortable saying "I don't understand" or "Tell me more about that."

Deep curiosity creates different conversations entirely. When customers sense your genuine interest, they open up. They share context, concerns, and complexities they wouldn't otherwise reveal. These conversations create real value and build trust that lasts far beyond any single transaction.

The Dimensions of Sales Curiosity

Excellence in sales requires curiosity in three distinct dimensions. Most salespeople develop strength in one or two, but excellence requires all three.

Customer Curiosity

This is curiosity about your customers, their businesses, challenges, goals, constraints, politics, and priorities. It is not just about their needs for your product. It is about truly understanding their world.

But customer curiosity has two dimensions: Curiosity about these issues from an organizational perspective and curiosity from an individual viewpoint. The first tends to look at facts, figures, strategics, goals, and data. The second focuses on the emotion or meaning of these things to the individuals we are engaging. How does what they do fit into the overall organizational goals? Where do they struggle? What does it mean to them?

We have to manage both simultaneously. And in complex B2B sales, we have to manage this across different parts of the organization and the entire buyer group.

The Organizational Dimension

The organizational dimension is what most salespeople focus on, and it's essential. We need to understand business drivers, strategic initiatives, competitive pressures, and financial constraints. These are the "what" and "why" at the enterprise level.

The Individual Dimension

But the individual dimension is where deals are often won or lost. And it's frequently overlooked. Every initiative, no matter how strategically sound, succeeds or fails based on the commitments and actions of individual people. And these people have concerns that transcend pure business logic: FOMU, the Fear Of Messing Up. Things like:

- Career implications: "If this succeeds, does it advance my career? If it fails, am I blamed?"

- Personal reputation: "What will my peers think? How does this reflect on my judgment?"
- Workload and disruption: "How much additional work will this create for me? Will it disrupt processes I've worked hard to establish?"
- Political positioning: "Who gains power or influence if this moves forward? Who loses?"
- Fear and insecurity: "Does this initiative make my role less essential? Could it expose gaps in my knowledge or skills?"

These individual concerns are often unspoken but enormously powerful. A procurement director might publicly support your solution while privately worrying that it makes their vendor relationships awkward. An operations manager might champion your proposal while secretly fearing that implementing it will make them look incompetent.

Top performers develop curiosity about both dimensions and understand how they intersect. They ask questions that reveal organizational priorities AND individual concerns. They listen for what's said and what's carefully not said. They build trust that allows people to voice their real worries, not just their official position.

Most importantly, they understand that supporting someone's success as an individual creates advocates who help drive organizational outcomes. When you genuinely care about how this decision affects someone's career, workload, and reputation, not just how it closes your deal, you create different conversations entirely.

The individual dimension of customer curiosity is ultimately about seeing your buyers as complex human beings with legitimate concerns, not just obstacles to navigate or boxes to check in your qualification process. It's about genuine empathy combined with business understanding.

Customer curiosity asks:

- What's really driving this initiative? What's the deeper why?
- What constraints are they operating under that they haven't explicitly stated?
- What does success look like from their perspective, not mine?
- What are they afraid of? What are they hoping for?
- How do their different stakeholders view this? Where might there be conflict?
- What does it mean to them, as individuals?

Market and Industry Curiosity

This is curiosity about the broader context in which your customers operate: industry trends, competitive dynamics, regulatory changes, technological disruptions, and market forces.

Top performers are students of their customers' industries. They read trade publications. They attend industry events. They understand the forces shaping their customers' worlds. They speak the language of the industry. This broader understanding allows them to have more strategic conversations, identify opportunities others miss, and provide insights customers truly value.

Self-Curiosity

This is curiosity about your own performance, behaviors, and development. It's the willingness to examine how you're doing, where you're falling short, and how you can improve.

Self-curiosity asks:

- Why did that conversation go the way it did? What could I have done differently?

- What patterns do I notice in my wins and losses?
- Where are my blind spots? What am I not seeing?
- What skills do I need to develop? What knowledge am I lacking?
- How are my beliefs and assumptions helping or hindering me?

In our work, I see this characteristic with top performers. Where we might be introducing a new process or initiative, most people resist. Top performers jump in with both feet. They try it out, test it, experiment. They make suggestions for improvement.

This form of curiosity is often the hardest. It requires honesty and vulnerability. But it's also the most powerful for long-term growth and development.

Cultivating Curiosity

Curiosity isn't entirely innate. While some people are naturally more curious than others, it's a capability that can be developed and strengthened. Here's how:

- Constantly challenge your assumptions: We all make assumptions about customers, situations, problems, and solutions. These assumptions are often invisible to us until we deliberately surface them. Practice identifying your assumptions and asking, "What if I'm wrong?" What else might be true? What am I missing?
- Embrace not knowing. Our business culture often treats "I don't know" as a weakness. It's the starting point for curiosity. Get comfortable with uncertainty. Practice saying, genuinely, "I don't know, help me understand." This invitation for explanation opens doors, driving deeper levels of conversation and learning.

- Ask better questions. Curiosity expresses itself through questions. But not all questions are equal. Move beyond yes/no questions and "Tell me about..." prompts. Move beyond the questions that serve your agenda. Ask questions that get at the why behind the what. Ask questions that reveal priorities, concerns, and context. Ask questions that make people think. Ask questions to invite others to ask questions. Most importantly, ask genuine questions, ones where you don't already know (or think you know) the answer.

- Listen to learn, not to respond. Curiosity requires genuine listening. Most of us listen while simultaneously formulating our response. We hear enough to know what we want to say next, then wait for our turn to speak. Genuine curiosity demands different listening; listening to understand, to discover, to learn. This means putting aside your agenda and truly focusing on what the other person is saying.

- Seek diverse perspectives. Curiosity withers in echo chambers. Actively seek out people who think differently from you. Read publications from different viewpoints. Talk to people in various roles, industries, and backgrounds. This diversity of input feeds curiosity and prevents the stagnation that comes from only reinforcing what you already believe.

Years ago, I was engaged by two different clients to look at innovation. One was a huge semiconductor company, the other a company in extreme sports. I suggested the two teams meet and share ideas. At first, they said, "How can anything in their business be useful for us? They are so different." But when we got together to exchange ideas, the semiconductor folks saw things the motorcycle racers were doing that could be tweaked and adapted to help them. And the motorcycle racers saw similar things.

The new perspectives and ideas had a profound impact on the projects each team was doing. The secret was looking in new and different places to find innovative ideas.

Make time for exploration. Curiosity needs time and space. You cannot be deeply curious while rushing from one activity to the next. Build time into your schedule for exploration. Whether that's researching an industry trend, diving deep into a customer's business, or reflecting on your own performance. This isn't wasted time; it is an investment in the very capability that separates top performers from the rest.

Questions That Change Everything

Here is something that might surprise you. Questions are a salesperson's best tool, but not because of the answers you get. They are powerful because of what they teach or what they enable people to imagine.

What is the best possible response I can get from asking a question? Someone saying, "You know, no one has ever asked me that before," or "Huh, I've never actually considered that." Those responses tell me I'm helping that customer look at things differently.

Good questions help customers identify gaps in their own understanding, see different points of view within their team, and remember things they might be forgetting.

Good questions provoke the customer to ask better, different questions of themselves.

Questions help the customer come up with better answers for themselves, not just answers for me.

And here's the key: it's not about the questions we need answered.

The questions that matter most are the ones that help the customer understand what they don't even know they don't know yet. Those are the questions they care about.

When we ask all the wrong questions, and all of us do it, we get exactly the answers we deserve.

Listening Beyond Learning: Making Others Feel Heard

There's a level of listening that transcends information gathering. Listening in a way that makes the other person feel truly heard. This is one of the most powerful yet underutilized capabilities in sales.

Most salespeople listen to extract information. They listen to qualify opportunities, understand needs, identify pain points, and gather facts they can use. This is listening to learn, and it matters. But it's incomplete.

Listening so others feel heard creates something fundamentally different: psychological safety, trust, and connection. It opens doors that purely transactional listening cannot.

The Difference Is Palpable

When someone is listening to extract information, you can feel it. They are waiting for their turn to speak. They interrupt when they hear what they need. They're mentally formulating their response before you finish. They steer the conversation back to their agenda. Their questions serve their needs, not yours.

When we are listening to extract information, we miss what is really being said. And these are the most important things!

When someone is listening so you feel heard, you feel that too. They are fully present. They don't interrupt or rush. They ask questions that help you think more clearly, not questions that advance their agenda. They reflect back what you have said to ensure they understand. They seem genuinely interested in your perspective, not just in how your perspective can be used.

The difference shows up in customer responses. When people feel heard, they:

Share more fully. They move beyond surface answers to genuine concerns and deeper context. They voice the worries they wouldn't usually mention. They trust you with information they carefully guard from others.

Think more clearly. The act of being heard helps people organize their own thinking. When someone truly listens without an agenda, it creates space for the speaker to process and clarify. You help them better understand their own situation.

Feel valued as individuals. Not as a means to your ends, but as people whose perspectives and concerns matter. This is the foundation of genuine partnership.

Become more open to influence. When people feel heard, they're more receptive to hearing you in return. Influence flows naturally from mutual understanding, not from clever persuasion techniques.

What Listening to Be Heard Looks Like

This kind of listening requires several shifts from typical sales listening:

Give your full attention. Not just passive attention, but active engagement. Put down your phone. Close your laptop. Stop thinking about your next meeting. Be completely present. If you are on a virtual call, close all other windows on your screen and ignore the "coaching" your latest AI tool might be giving you. Be totally present. People sense when you're truly attentive versus merely polite.

Listen without an agenda. This doesn't mean having no purpose for the conversation. It means temporarily setting aside your goal of advancing the sale to create genuine space for understanding. The irony: the less you push your agenda, the more effectively you advance it.

Ask questions that serve them, not you. "What are you most worried about?" serves them. "When can you make a decision?" serves you. "What would success look like from your perspective?" serves them. "What's your budget?" serves you. The difference isn't subtle.

Reflect and confirm understanding. "What I'm hearing is..." or "It sounds like you're concerned about..." or "So the key issue from your perspective is..." These phrases do two things: they ensure you've understood correctly, and they demonstrate you've been listening carefully. Both build trust.

Follow their thread, not yours. When someone shares something that matters to them, explore it deeper before redirecting. Don't treat their concerns as items to check off so you can get back to your message. Their concerns ARE the conversation.

Validate without agreeing. You can acknowledge someone's concerns as legitimate even when you think they're overblown. "I understand why that would be concerning" or "That makes sense given your experience" shows respect for their perspective without requiring you to agree with their conclusion.

Create silence. After someone finishes speaking, pause. Count to three in your head. Often, the most crucial thing they have to say comes after they think they're finished. But only if you create space for it. Don't rush to fill the silence.

Why This Matters Beyond Technique

Listening so others feel heard is not a sales technique. It's an expression of respect and genuine curiosity about other people. When deployed as a mere technique, when you fake it, it rings hollow and damages trust more than not trying at all.

This kind of listening is also challenging because it requires setting aside your ego and your immediate goals. You must be genuinely interested in understanding their world, even when that understanding does not immediately serve your needs.

But what's powerful: when you consistently listen this way, several things happen:

You earn the right to challenge. People accept challenges from those who've demonstrated they understand. When you've truly heard someone, they're open to hearing you push back on their thinking.

You uncover the real issues. The concerns people voice initially are often not their actual concerns. When they feel heard, they eventually share what they're really worried about, and that's where you can actually help.

You build loyalty that transcends transactions. People remember how you make them feel. When you are one of the few who truly listen, you become someone they want to work with, regardless of product features or pricing.

You become a thinking partner, not a vendor. Vendors are interchangeable. Thinking partners are irreplaceable. The difference often comes down to listening quality.

The Connection to Customer-Centricity

Listening so others feel heard is perhaps the purest expression of customer-centricity. It says, through action, not words, "Your perspective matters. Your concerns are legitimate. You are not just a means to my commission but a person worthy of genuine understanding."

This doesn't mean abandoning your goals or becoming a therapist. It means recognizing that the fastest path to your goals often runs through a genuine understanding of theirs. And that genuine understanding requires listening that goes beyond information extraction to creating an experience of being heard.

In a world where everyone is rushing, where most conversations feel transactional, and where people rarely feel truly heard, this capability becomes a profound competitive advantage. Not because it's a clever tactic, but because it reflects the kind of person and partner customers want to work with.

Reflection Exercises

These exercises will help you assess and develop your curiosity across all three dimensions:

- **Rate your curiosity**: On a scale of 1-10, how curious are you in each dimension? Customer curiosity? Market/industry curiosity? Self-curiosity? Which dimension is strongest? Which needs the most development?

- Examine your last customer conversation, watch the recording, look at the transcript: Were your questions genuine or perfunctory? Did you truly listen or wait to respond? What did you learn that you didn't expect? What did you fail to learn that you should have? What did your customer learn that they didn't expect?

- **Identify your assumptions:** Pick one of your active opportunities. List every assumption you're making about it. About the customer's needs, priorities, constraints, decision process, timeline, budget, and politics. Now challenge each one. How do you know it's true? What if you're wrong?

- **Assess your learning habits:** How much time do you spend learning about your customers' industries versus learning about your products? What industry publications do you read? What trends are you tracking? What do you need to know that you currently don't?

- **Practice self-reflection:** Review your last lost deal. Go beyond the surface explanation. What didn't you understand that you should have? What assumptions did you make that were wrong? What questions didn't you ask? What patterns from previous losses do you see repeating?

(The complementary AI tools will help with this reflection exercise.)

For Sales Leaders: Cultivating Curiosity in Your Team

Curiosity can't be mandated, but it can be cultivated. As a leader, you have tremendous influence over whether curiosity thrives or withers in your organization.

Why Curiosity Dies in Sales Organizations

Before you can cultivate curiosity, understand what kills it. Be honest: Are you inadvertently creating a culture that suppresses curiosity?

Curiosity-killing leadership behaviors:

- Providing scripts and requiring strict adherence to them.
- Measuring only volume metrics (calls, meetings), not quality or outcomes.
- Punishing or criticizing people for asking "why."
- Never asking curious questions yourself in team meetings.
- Accepting surface-level answers in pipeline reviews.
- Creating such intense time pressure that exploration becomes impossible.

Model Deep Curiosity

Your team learns what you value by watching what you do. If you want curious salespeople, you must be a curious leader.

Demonstrate curiosity by:

- Asking "why" and "how" questions in every pipeline review, not just "what" and "when."
- Admitting when you don't know something and modeling the process of finding out.
- Sharing interesting things you've learned about your customers' industries.
- Actively and genuinely seeking their ideas, input, and feedback.
- Asking your team questions that make them think, not just questions to test their knowledge.

Encourage your team to ask each other and your questions that make everyone think.

Being genuinely interested in your team members' perspectives and experiences.

Creating Space for Curiosity

Curiosity requires time and psychological safety. Create both.

Time:

- Build research and preparation time into expectations.
- Don't schedule every minute. Allow for exploration and learning.
- Reward quality of interaction, not just volume.

Psychological safety:

- Welcome questions and challenges from your team.
- Never punish "I don't know" when it's said honestly.
- Celebrate when someone discovers something new about a customer.
- Frame losses as learning opportunities, not just failures.

Coaching for Curiosity

Transform your one-on-ones and coaching sessions into curiosity development opportunities:

- After deal reviews, ask: "What did you learn about this customer that surprised you?"
- Challenge assumptions: "How do you know that? What if that assumption is wrong?"
- Encourage deeper exploration: "What questions haven't you asked yet?"

- Model better questions by asking them, then discussing why those questions matter

Questions for Leaders

- How curious are you as a leader? When was the last time you learned something genuinely new about your customers' industries?
- What percentage of questions in your last pipeline review were genuinely curious versus checking for information you already expected? Do your metrics and incentives reward curiosity or volume? What would need to change?
- When was the last time someone on your team asked you a question that made you think differently? What does that tell you?
- If you were brutally honest, are you creating a culture that cultivates or kills curiosity?

A Story From The Field, One Question

A seller had been working on a deal for six months. He had a critical call on the key executive. While unusual, he asked me to participate in the meeting.

We were 10 minutes into the meeting; I knew the problem. He was pitching features while the customer nodded politely.

During a pause, I asked: "I'm curious, what happens if you don't solve this problem in the next six months?"

The customer looked at the ceiling, then back at me. "You know what? I honestly don't know. We've been so focused on the solution that we never talked about what happens if we don't fix this."

That one question opened up thirty minutes of conversation about real business impact: customer churn, employee morale, and a competitor gaining ground. The deal closed two weeks later.

Most sellers stop being curious once they think they understand the problem. They move into solution mode. But the real insights, the ones that actually move deals forward, come from staying curious just a little bit longer.

Chapter 3
The Commitment to Continuous Learning

"Anyone who stops learning is old, whether at twenty or eighty. Anyone who keeps learning stays young." Henry Ford

The Learning Crisis in Sales

There is a troubling pattern in sales organizations: most learning stops after initial onboarding. Sure, salespeople attend the occasional training session or webinar. They might skim industry articles. But genuine, sustained, purposeful learning? It's rare.

This creates a dangerous stagnation. The world changes rapidly; customer expectations evolve, technologies appear, competitive dynamics shift, and best practices advance. If you're not continuously learning, you are falling behind. Not staying in place but actually falling behind.

Consider two salespeople hired at the same time with identical skills. Five years later, one invested in continuous learning while the other relied solely on their initial training. The gap between them isn't incremental; it's exponential. The learner has compounded their capabilities year after year. The non-learner hasn't just stood still; in a changing environment, standing still means moving backward.

Why Learning Stops

We are Focusing on the Wrong 10%!

A colleague shared fascinating research with me about how people learn. Only 10% of learning comes through formal training programs. Another 20% comes through observation and feedback. And the remaining 70%? That comes through real-world experience.

Think about that for a second. We focus most of our time and dollars on the part that has the least impact on learning. Now, when I work with companies on training programs, I spend a ton of time asking, "Okay, so what are you going to do to make sure people actually apply this stuff? How will they practice? How will they improve their capabilities after our training program ends? How will you continually coach and reinforce it?"

If we really want sales training to make a difference, we've got to focus on two things: First, how do we embed the skills into everyday practice so salespeople can truly learn by applying them? And second, how do we watch what they're doing and give them feedback? Without ongoing feedback and coaching, development won't happen fast enough. Athletes and musicians get this. They improve most through constant, disciplined practice. And the best ones always make sure they've got outstanding coaches who give them feedback to help them reach the highest levels of performance.

If learning is so important, why does it stop? Several factors contribute:

- **The illusion of competence.** Once you've achieved basic competence in sales, it's easy to believe you know enough. You can execute the fundamental activities. You occasionally hit your numbers. This feels like mastery, but it's just baseline proficiency. The gap between competence and excellence is vast, and it's filled with continuous learning.
- **The busyness trap.** You're too busy to learn. There's always another call to make, another email to send, another meeting to attend. Learning feels like a luxury you can't afford. But this

thinking is backwards. Learning is the investment that makes everything else more effective. You are not too busy to learn; you're too busy because you are not learning.

- **The fixed mindset**. Some people believe abilities are largely fixed. You are either naturally good at sales, or you're not. This fixed mindset kills learning. Why invest in development if your capabilities are predetermined? The truth is that excellence in sales, like most things, is developed through deliberate practice and continuous learning, not bestowed by genetics.

- **Unclear learning priorities**. With so many things to learn, many people learn nothing. Without clear direction on what matters most for their development, they default to random, sporadic learning that produces minimal results. Or they avoid learning entirely, paralyzed by too many options.

Fixed vs. Growth Mindset

Your beliefs about learning fundamentally shape your trajectory. Carol Dweck's research on mindsets reveals two distinct approaches.

Fixed Mindset:

- Believes abilities are innate and essentially unchangeable. (Think of all the stories about "salespeople are born, not made.")
- Avoids challenges that might expose limitations.
- Views effort as evidence of insufficient natural ability.
- Takes feedback personally and defensively.
- Feels threatened by others' success.

Growth Mindset:

- Believes abilities can be developed through dedication and work.
- Embraces challenges as opportunities to improve.
- Sees effort as the path to mastery.
- Treats feedback as valuable information for improvement.
- Finds inspiration in others' success.

The growth mindset isn't naive optimism. It's not believing you can be anything you want, regardless of circumstances. It's recognizing that you have far more capacity for development than you realize, and that sustained effort in the right direction produces real growth.

Growth Mindset in a Dynamic Environment

There's another dimension to a growth mindset that's particularly relevant for sales professionals: understanding that the environment itself is dynamic, and what worked yesterday may not work tomorrow.

Many salespeople plateau not because they stop learning, but because they keep learning the same things over and over. They refine last year's approaches. They get incrementally better at tactics that are becoming less relevant. They achieve mastery of methods that the market is leaving behind.

A true growth mindset in sales must include environmental awareness: no matter how good you are today, tomorrow will be different if you don't adjust to new market dynamics.

The Dynamic Environment Reality

Consider what's changed in just the past few years:

Buyer behavior has fundamentally shifted. The percentage of the buying process completed before engaging sellers continues to increase. Decision-making has become more consensus driven. Buyers expect sellers to bring insights they couldn't find through their own research.

Technology has reshaped everything. AI tools are changing how both buyers and sellers work. Remote selling has become permanent. Digital channels have proliferated. The tools that were competitive advantages last year are table stakes today.

Competition has intensified. New business models disrupt established ones. Companies from adjacent industries enter your market. "We've always done it this way" is a death sentence.

Customer expectations keep rising. What delighted customers three years ago is merely acceptable today. The bar for "good enough" keeps rising.

In this environment, a growth mindset means more than believing you can improve. It means recognizing that continuous adaptation is not optional. Your choice is not whether to change, but whether you'll change proactively (while maintaining control) or reactively (under pressure).

From Learning to Adapting

Learning without putting what has been learned into action is wasted effort. This environmental dimension of growth mindset requires several shifts:

- **From optimization to reimagination.** Don't just ask "How can I do this better?" Ask "Should I still be doing this at all? Is there a fundamentally different approach that fits the new environment?"

- **From skill development to capability evolution.** Yesterday's skills included prospecting and presenting. Today's essential capabilities include facilitating buying processes and orchestrating virtual consensus. Tomorrow's requirements will still be different.

- **From best practices to contextual judgment.** Best practices encode what worked in past conditions. A growth mindset means knowing when to follow them and when to abandon them based on the current context.

- **From incremental improvement to transformative shifts.** Sometimes you need to make incremental progress. Sometimes you need to discard your approach entirely and start fresh. A growth mindset includes the wisdom to know what is required.

I have a confession to make. I have two small tattoos. On my left arm, it says "Obsessive Learning." On the right, it says "Relentless Execution." Those are constant reminders to me. And they go hand in hand; both are required for growth and success.

Curiosity as the Bridge

This is where curiosity and a growth mindset intersect powerfully. Curiosity about your customers' changing situations, market dynamics, and emerging best practices reveals what you need to learn next.

The salespeople who thrive through market shifts aren't necessarily the ones who learn fastest. They're the ones whose curiosity about the changing environment helps them understand the right things at the right time.

A growth mindset without environmental awareness creates people who are excellent at things that no longer matter. Environmental awareness without a growth mindset makes people who see the need to change but don't believe they can.

Together, they create professionals who can continuously adjust to serve customers effectively, regardless of how the market shifts. That's the kind of resilience excellence requires.

The Three Domains of Sales Learning

Effective learning in sales spans three interconnected domains. Excellence requires ongoing development in all three:

1. Skills and Techniques.

This is the "how" of selling. The specific capabilities and methods you use. Prospecting approaches, qualification frameworks, negotiation techniques, and presentation skills. These are learnable, improvable skills. Top performers never stop refining their technique. They study what works, experiment with variations, and continuously improve their craft.

2. Knowledge and Expertise

This is the "what" of selling. The substance you bring to conversations. Industry knowledge, business acumen, understanding of customer challenges, awareness of trends and forces shaping the customer's world. This isn't product knowledge (though that matters too), it is the deep understanding of them and their business that allows you to be truly valuable.

Imagine engaging a customer without talking about what you sell, even if they ask you. You must focus on them and their business. But this is what they really care about and where they struggle most.

The ability to do this requires constant learning and updating as customers and industries change.

3. Self-Awareness and Mindset

Understanding yourself, your patterns, strengths, weaknesses, blind spots, and the beliefs driving your behaviors. This is perhaps the most important and most neglected domain of learning. You can't improve what you don't understand about yourself.

Most training focuses exclusively on domain one (skills). Some include domain two (knowledge). Almost none address domain three (self-awareness). Yet without self-awareness, skills and expertise have limited impact. You'll keep repeating the same patterns, hitting the same walls, making the same mistakes.

Learning from Every Experience

The most powerful learning doesn't come from courses or books. It comes from extracting lessons from daily experience. Every customer interaction, every win, every loss, every challenge contains valuable learning if you're paying attention.

- **Learning from wins:** Most people celebrate wins and then move on. High performers analyze them. What specifically contributed to this success? What did you do differently? What did the customer respond to? What assumptions proved correct? What can you replicate? Wins have patterns worth understanding and repeating.

- **Learning from losses:** Losses hurt, which is why most people avoid analyzing them deeply. But losses are often more instructive than wins. What did you miss? What assumptions were wrong? Where did you lose the customer? What did the winner do differently? The painful honesty of loss analysis accelerates learning more than anything else.

- **Learning from everyday interactions:** Not just major deals, every customer conversation offers learning. What question worked well? What approach fell flat? What did you learn about this customer or their industry? What would you do differently next time? This habit of extracting learning from every interaction compounds rapidly.

Building a Personal Learning System

Random, sporadic learning produces random, sporadic results. Excellence requires a system. A deliberate approach to continuous development. Here is how to build one:

1. Identify your learning priorities. You can't learn everything. Focus on what matters most for your next level of performance. Where are your most significant gaps? What skills would have the highest impact? What knowledge would make you most valuable to customers? Choose no more than three priorities at a time and concentrate your learning energy there.
2. Create a learning rhythm. Make learning regular and predictable. This might be 30 minutes each morning reading industry news, Friday afternoons reviewing the week's lessons, and one hour weekly for a deep dive learning session on a priority topic. The specific rhythm matters less than having one and sticking to it, consistency compounds.

3. Diversify your learning sources.   Books, articles, podcasts, courses, conferences, peer conversations, customer interactions, mentors. Each offers a different value. Don't rely on a single source. The interplay between different inputs creates a richer understanding than any single source provides.

4. Practice deliberately.   Learning is not just about consuming information. It's about application and practice. Please take what you learn and deliberately practice it. Try innovative approaches in low-stakes situations first. Reflect on what works. Adjust and try again. This cycle of learning-applying-reflecting-adjusting is where real skill development happens.

5. Capture and review insights.   Don't let learning evaporate. Capture key insights in whatever system works for you: notes, journal, digital app. Periodically review what you have learned. The act of review reinforces learning and helps you notice patterns you might have missed.

What Makes the Great Ones Great

Great salespeople are curious about the profession of selling itself. They're constantly learning, improving, and changing things up.

They never think they have learned everything; they are always interested in seeing what other successful people are doing, both in their own companies and in other organizations.

They are constantly pushing themselves, trying new things, running experiments, and always looking to get better.

You know what's great about hiring curious salespeople? It makes life so much easier for managers. Look, it's impossible to train people in everything they need to know. There's just too much. But curious salespeople will figure out they've got gaps in their knowledge, and they'll go fill those gaps themselves.

They'll constantly re-examine their strategies, always trying to improve them. By their very nature, they're challengers. They'll challenge their customers about why they do things a certain way and whether they've considered doing something else.

The Compound Effect of Learning

Learning compounds like interest. Each new insight builds on previous learning, creating accelerating returns. Someone who commits to just 30 minutes of focused learning daily accumulates over 180 hours per year, -equivalent to more than four full work weeks of dedicated development time.

But the real power isn't just in the hours, it's in the compounding. As you learn, you develop better mental models for understanding new information. You make connections faster. You see patterns others miss. You apply insights more effectively. Learning itself makes you a better learner.

Over time, this creates massive divergence in capability. Two people who start in the same place can end up in completely different leagues based solely on their commitment to continuous learning. The gap isn't talent-it's the accumulated impact of one person learning while the other does not.

Remember, if you get just 1% better each day, by the end of the year, you will be 37.8 times better than where you started!

Overcoming Learning Obstacles

Even with commitment, obstacles arise. Here's how to address the most common ones:

Obstacle: No time!

Solution: Learning doesn't require large blocks of time. Fifteen minutes here, twenty minutes there; it adds up. Listen to podcasts during commutes. Read articles while waiting for meetings. The question is not "Do I have time?" but "Is this a priority?"

Obstacle: Don't know what to learn!

Solution: Start with gaps. What skill do you struggle with? What knowledge would help you win more deals? What feedback do you consistently receive? What is the one thing that you hope your customer never asks? Your current performance issues are excellent guides for learning priorities.

Obstacle: Overwhelmed by options!

Solution: Focus narrowly. Choose one skill and one knowledge domain. Master those before expanding. Depth beats breadth when building capability.

Obstacle: Learning doesn't stick.

Solution: Apply immediately. Learning without application evaporates quickly. Take one insight from every learning session and use it that day. Application cements learning.

Skating to Where the Puck Is Going

Wayne Gretzky has this famous quote: "I skate to where the puck is going to be, not where it is." Yeah, it's become a bit of a cliché, but it's still brilliant. The problem is, when I talk to executives and salespeople about the skills and competencies that matter for sales success, I get the feeling we're all focused on where the puck is right now.

Most of what we look for when we're recruiting and what we train people on are the classic sales competencies: prospecting, questioning, listening, objection handling, closing, deal management, pipeline management, and account management. You get the idea.

Those were the exact same skills and competencies my managers were looking for when I was hired into my first professional sales role decades ago.

We need to start equipping people with the skills that'll matter in the coming years: critical thinking and problem solving, project management, collaboration and team leadership, change management, and genuine business acumen.

We need people who are comfortable with ambiguity and uncertainty. People who are creative and curious. People who are mentally tough and self-directed. We need to look forward, not backward.

.... And Then The AI Factor....

And all of this has never been more important. We are in the early days of one of the most transformative technologies the world has ever experienced, AI. This technology changes everything, and we will still be figuring this out for years. But if we aren't curious, if we don't have an open mindset, if we aren't continuously learning, we will miss the genuine growth opportunity.

Too much of our focus on AI is skating to where the puck currently is. We use these tools to do the same work we have traditionally done, perhaps much faster, maybe a little smarter. But we are still basically doing the same things we have always done.

But we have the opportunity to learn, to experiment, to try new things. We have the opportunity to completely reimagine how our work gets done and how our customers' work gets done.

We have the opportunity to reinvent ourselves, our organizations completely, and how we create value with our customers, in our markets, and in our communities.

In writing this book, you can see how I am trying to practice what I preach. I profoundly believe that AI helps us imagine new ways of creating learning and growth experiences for my audience. Choosing Claude as my co-author and experimenting with developing and writing a book are changing how I think. Developing the AI tools that accompany this book takes that learning-putting-into-practice cycle even further.

Reflection Exercises

These exercises will help you build a sustainable learning practice.

- **Assess your mindset**: Do you have a fixed or growth mindset about sales capabilities? What evidence supports your answer? How does your mindset affect your learning behavior?
- **Calculate your learning time:** How many hours did you spend on purposeful learning last month? Not training you were required to attend, rather deliberate learning you chose to pursue. What does this number tell you?
- **Identify your learning priorities:** What are the 2-3 skills or knowledge areas that would most impact your performance? Why these specifically?
- **Map your learning sources:** Where do you currently learn? What sources are missing that could be valuable? What would varying your sources require?
- **Design your learning rhythm:** What specific learning activities will you do daily? Weekly? Monthly? Be concrete: what, when, where, how long?

- **Analyze a recent loss:** Pick a deal you lost recently. Go deep: What didn't you understand? What skills were lacking? What would you need to learn to have won? What will you learn from this?

(The complementary AI tools will help with this reflection exercise.)

For Sales Leaders: Building a Learning Culture

Organizations don't learn; people do. Your role is creating the conditions where learning thrives and is valued.

Why Most Sales Organizations Don't Learn

Despite spending millions on training, most sales organizations aren't learning organizations. They are training organizations, which are quite different. Training is episodic and event based. Learning is continuous and integrated into daily work.

Let me look at this issue again. The "half-life" of training, based on research, is between 9 and 21 days. What this means is that we are spending millions on training, only to lose most of that investment within a few weeks.

How do we reverse this? We must move from event-based training to learning. After a training program, we have to continuously reinforce the training, coach, and continue developing skills until they have become internalized or habits.

Signs your organization isn't learning:

- Same mistakes repeated across the team and over time.
- Learning happens only in formal training sessions.

- No systematic capture or sharing of lessons learned.
- People are punished for admitting what they don't know.
- No time allocated for learning and development.

Model Continuous Learning

You set the tone. If you are not visibly learning, why would your team prioritize it?

Demonstrate learning by:

- Regularly sharing what you are learning-books, articles, insights from customers
- Admitting when you don't know something and showing how you find out.
- Asking your team to teach you things they know.
- Visibly investing in your own development.
- Talking about your learning process, not just results.

Integrate Learning into Daily Work

Do not treat learning as separate from work. Make it integral:

- Start meetings with "What did we learn this week?"
- Transform pipeline reviews into learning sessions-analyze patterns, share insights.
- After wins and losses, facilitate learning discussions, not just post-mortems.
- Create peer learning forums where team members share expertise.
- Put learning into practice. Without constant practice and refinement, learning will never be retained.

- Build reflection time into schedules-not every minute should be "productive activity."

Support Individual Learning Journeys

Each person on your team has unique development needs. Support them:

- Help each person identify their learning priorities based on their goals and gaps.
- Provide resources-books, courses, conference attendance, tools, coaching.
- Hold people accountable for their learning commitments, just like you do for quotas.
- Celebrate learning milestones and skill development publicly.
- Connect learning to career progression-show that development leads to opportunity.

Questions for Leaders

- What did you personally learn last week? If you can't answer easily, what does that tell you about your modeling?
- How much time does your team spend on learning versus executing? What's the right balance?
- What organizational barriers make learning difficult for your team? What can you remove?
- When was the last time someone on your team told you about something new they learned? What does the frequency tell you?
- If you could wave a magic wand and change one thing to create a stronger learning culture, what would it be? What is stopping you from doing that now?

A Story From The Field, The $150,000 Autopsy

Early in my career, I lost a deal that should have been mine. We had the best solution, the best relationship, and I thought the deal was wrapped up. Then we lost to a competitor I'd never even considered a threat. I was devastated and wanted to move on quickly.

My manager insisted I do a post-mortem. We sat down; I was embarrassed to discover I'd spent six months selling to the wrong person, someone I thought was the decision-maker wasn't.

She asked me to sit down and think about what went wrong. I spent three hours documenting everything I'd learned and created a checklist. That loss cost me about $150,000 in commission. But those lessons have made me tens of millions over my career.

Most people try to ignore or forget those losses, putting them behind them. Top performers treat them like treasure maps. The question is: Are you learning, or are you just moving on?

Chapter 4
Personal Accountability-No Excuses, Just Results

"Accountability is the glue that ties commitment to results."
Bob Proctor

The Accountability Crisis

When did it become acceptable to blame everyone and everything else for our results? Scan through any pipeline review, any performance discussion, any deal debrief, and you'll hear a litany of excuses: "The leads marketing gives me aren't any good; My territory is the worst; The product isn't competitive; Pricing is too high; The economy is terrible right now; Customers just aren't buying!"

All of these might contain kernels of truth. But they're also deflections-ways of avoiding the central question: What could I have done differently?

The uncomfortable truth is that in most organizations, excuses have become normalized. We have created cultures where explaining away poor performance is not only accepted but expected. Managers ask for the story behind the numbers, and sellers provide detailed narratives about all the external factors that prevented success.

This is killing performance.

There's Always Going to Be an Excuse

I was listening to my friend Matt Heinz on a podcast, and he said something so obvious yet so profound: "Every day there is an excuse." It's such an astute observation!

There has always been and always will be any number of reasons to make excuses. We've seen rapid change and disruption create all sorts of new excuses. This week it might be global economic turmoil. Then there's AI, everyone's favorite excuse these days.

But we create plenty of other excuses. Our products aren't competitive enough. We don't have enough people. We don't have the right people. Our pricing isn't competitive. The goals are unreasonable. We don't have the right tools and technology.

And then there is the ultimate excuse, it's the customers! They don't get it, they don't understand, they can't find the money to buy what we're selling. Occasionally, I even hear a salesperson say, "The dog ate my pipeline report!" OK, maybe I'm kidding on that one.

Look, if you don't care about what you are doing, if you don't care about what you can learn and achieve, you're wasting your time and everyone else's. Find something you're enthusiastic about because excuses are just that, excuses. If you want to learn, grow, and achieve something, excuses won't get you there.

Responsibility vs. Accountability

These terms are often used interchangeably, but they are fundamentally different:

Responsibility: Responsibility is about your role and duties. It is what you're supposed to do-your job description, your assigned tasks, your territory, your quota. Responsibility is external. It is assigned to you by others.

Accountability: Accountability is about ownership. It is internal. It's the commitment you make to yourself to meet your obligations, regardless of circumstances. You cannot be made accountable-you must choose it.

Here is the critical distinction: You can be responsible for something without being accountable for it. You can execute your responsibilities grudgingly, making excuses when results don't materialize. Or you can own them fully, taking accountability not just for activities but for outcomes.

Excellence requires accountability, not just responsibility.

A Note on Definitions:

You may be familiar with RACI (Responsible, Accountable, Consult, Inform), the project management framework where these terms have specific technical meanings. In RACI, "Responsible" refers to who does the work and "Accountable" refers to who approves it.

Our usage here is different and more fundamental. We are discussing these as personal mindsets rather than project roles: responsibility as the external obligation you're given, and accountability as the internal commitment you choose to make. Neither definition is "right" or "wrong." They serve different purposes. For our discussion of mindset and personal excellence, this distinction between external assignment and internal ownership is what matters most.

The Anatomy of an Excuse

Excuses follow predictable patterns. Understanding these patterns helps you recognize-and stop-excuse-making behavior:

- **External Attribution:** "It's not my fault because [external factor]." This places the locus of control outside yourself. The territory, the leads, the product, the market-anything but you. While external factors exist, this mindset renders you powerless. If success depends entirely on external factors, you have no agency.

- **Selective Evidence:** "Look at all these things working against me." This cherry-picks data that supports the excuse while ignoring contradictory evidence. Yes, your territory is challenging-but someone else with a similar territory is succeeding. The question isn't whether obstacles exist, but how you respond to them.

- **Comparison to Ideal:** "If only I had [ideal circumstances]." This compares your reality to an imagined perfect scenario. If only you had better leads, a better territory, a better product, lower pricing-then you'd succeed. This thinking is useless because you don't operate in ideal circumstances. Nobody does. The question is: How do you excel within actual circumstances?

Stop Creating Excuses

There is another category of excuses I hear all the time: "I need an excuse to get back into the customer." Creating excuses to get back to the customer is nothing but old sales mythology. It does nothing to serve us or the customer.

We are all desperate to find customers willing to talk to us. Once we find them, we won't let go. We want any excuse to keep having meetings. This just takes time, our time and the customers'.

We should stop creating excuses to see the customer. Each meeting needs to be focused and purposeful. Both the customer and we are better off with fewer but impactful meetings, not unnecessary meetings.

Getting back into the customer is never a problem if you create value in every interchange. They will always be willing to see you because of that value. You only need excuses when you stop creating value.

The Cost of Excuses

Excuses feel protective in the moment. They shield your ego from the pain of failure. But this protection comes at a steep price:

For you personally:

- You learn nothing. Excuses prevent the honest analysis necessary for improvement.
- You become powerless. If results are always someone else's fault, you have no control.
- Trust erodes. People stop believing you and stop giving you opportunities.
- Your skills atrophy. Without accountability for results, there's no pressure to improve.
- Careers stagnate. Organizations don't promote excuse-makers.

For your team and organization:

- Problems don't get solved. If nobody owns results, nothing improves.
- Culture degrades. Excuse-making is contagious and spreads quickly.
- Performance declines. Accountability drives results; excuses prevent them.
- Best performers leave. Top talent won't stay in cultures that tolerate mediocrity.

The Ownership Mindset

Moving from excuses to accountability requires a fundamental shift in how you view your role and results. The ownership mindset includes:

Extreme Ownership:

This concept, popularized by Jocko Willink and Leif Babin, means taking complete responsibility for everything in your world. Not just the things directly under your control, but everything that affects your outcomes.

- Bad leads? Own it. What could you do differently in prospecting? How could you work with marketing to improve lead quality? What can you control in this situation?
- Product deficiencies? So what! No one has the perfect product. Our customers don't expect the perfect product. In fact, they probably will only use a fraction of the product capabilities.

This does not mean external factors don't exist. It means you refuse to use them as excuses. You must figure out how to continue to move forward, overcoming obstacles. You focus entirely on what you can control and influence.

The Control Dichotomy

Distinguish clearly between what you can control, what you can influence, and what is truly outside your sphere:

- **Control:** Your actions, your preparation, your attitude, your effort, your choices.

- **Influence:** Customer perception, team collaboration, internal priorities, market positioning.
- **Outside:** Market conditions, competitor actions, economic factors, organizational decisions.

Accountability means maximizing what you control, leveraging what you can influence, and refusing to dwell on what's outside your sphere.

"What Can I Do Differently?"

This is the accountability question. Not "Why didn't this work? or Whose fault is this?" but "What can I do differently?"

This question assumes agency. It presumes you have options, choices, and influence. It redirects energy from blame to problem-solving. It is uncomfortable because it eliminates excuses, but it's also empowering because it puts you in control.

The Path to Accountability

Building genuine accountability isn't about forced confession or public flogging. It's about creating internal commitment and external structure that supports ownership:

Make Explicit Commitments

Accountability begins with clarity. You cannot be accountable for vague aspirations. Make specific, measurable commitments:

- Not "I'll do better at prospecting," but "I will have 10 quality conversations with prospects in my ICP this week."

- Not "I'll work on this deal" but "By Friday, I will have a meeting with the economic buyer and understand their three top priorities."

Clear commitments create clear accountability.

Own the Outcomes

When you meet your commitment, acknowledge it. When you don't, own that too, without making excuses. "I committed to X and achieved Y" is accountability. "I committed to X but couldn't because..." is excuse-making.

This does not mean you don't explain context. But explanation is different from excuses. Explanation says: "Here's what happened, Here's what I learned, and Here's what I need to change." Excuse says: "Here's why it wasn't my fault."

Learn from Every Failure

Accountability is not about never failing. It's about owning failures and extracting lessons from them. After every miss, every loss, every shortfall, ask:

- What specifically went wrong?
- What did I control that I could have done differently?
- What assumptions did I make that proved incorrect?
- What will I do differently next time?

These questions are painful but powerful. They're how you grow.

Build External Accountability

Self-accountability is important but insufficient. We are all prone to self-deception. Build external accountability:

- Share commitments with your manager, peers, or a mentor.
- Report on progress regularly, honestly.
- Invite feedback and challenge.
- Create consequences for yourself when you don't meet commitments.

External accountability keeps you honest when internal motivation wanes.

Celebrate Ownership

When you demonstrate accountability-when you own a mistake, when you focus on what you can control, when you skip the excuses-acknowledge it. This positive reinforcement strengthens the accountability muscle.

Reflection Exercises

- **Examine your language:** Review your last week of communications (emails, CRM notes, conversations). Count how many times you attributed results to external factors versus your own actions. What's the ratio? A small team I managed created a game with this. Every time they made an excuse, they tossed a dollar into a jar. The person with the fewest excuses each week won everything in the jar. You can imagine how natural competitiveness reduced the number of excuses quickly.

- **Identify your favorite excuses:** What explanations do you routinely use for subpar performance? Be honest. Write them down. Now challenge each one: What could you control or influence in these situations?
- **Analyze a recent shortfall:** Pick something you did not achieve recently. Write two versions: Version 1: All the external factors that contributed. Version 2: Everything you could have done differently. Which version is longer? Which is more useful for future performance?
- **Define your commitments:** What specific, measurable commitments are you making for the next 30 days? Write them down. Share them with someone who will hold you accountable.
- **Practice ownership language**: For one week, eliminate explanatory language about external factors. When something doesn't go well, start with "I" not "they" or "it." Notice how this shift in language changes your thinking.

(The complementary AI tools will help with this reflection exercise.)

For Sales Leaders: Creating Accountable Teams

You can't make people accountable. But you can create conditions where accountability thrives or withers. Most organizations inadvertently enable excuse-making.

Stop Accepting Excuses

The most important thing you can do, stop accepting excuses. Not harshly or punitively, but clearly. When someone offers an excuse, redirect: "I understand those challenges exist. Set those aside for a moment-what could you have done differently?"

This is not about being unsympathetic. It is about maintaining a standard. If you accept excuses, you are teaching people that excuses are acceptable.

Model Accountability

When you miss a commitment, own it. When something goes wrong, take responsibility. When your team underperforms, resist the urge to blame them or external factors. Ask yourself first: "What could I have done differently as their leader?"

Your team mirrors your behavior. If you make excuses, they will make excuses. If you demonstrate ownership, they will follow.

Create Clarity

People can't be accountable for unclear expectations. Ensure everyone knows:

- Exactly what they are accountable for (not just activity, but outcomes).
- How success is measured.
- What resources and support are available?
- What consequences exist for not meeting commitments?

Ambiguity is the enemy of accountability.

Address Legitimate Barriers

Sometimes the obstacles people cite are real and significant. When that's true, work with them to remove barriers or find workarounds. But distinguish between "This makes things harder" and "This makes things impossible."

Most barriers make things harder. Accountability means succeeding despite difficulty.

Recognition and Consequences. Recognize and reward accountability, especially when someone owns a mistake or takes responsibility for poor results. This courage should be celebrated.

Conversely, there must be consequences for persistent excuse-making. Not punishment, but honest conversations about whether this role or organization is right for someone who won't take ownership.

Questions for Leaders

- When was the last time you accepted an excuse from someone on your team? What did that teach them?
- When was the last time you owned a mistake without explanation or excuse? What did that demonstrate to your team?
- Are your expectations clear enough that people know exactly what they are accountable for? How do you know?
- Who on your team consistently makes excuses? What conversation do you need to have with them?
- What systems or processes create legitimate barriers to your team's success? What can you change?

A Story From The Field, The Excuse Artist

I once had a seller who could have won a gold medal in excuse-making. Every forecast call was a masterclass: "The CFO went on vacation, procurement changed requirements, the champion left, the budget got frozen." Every excuse was technically valid. But I noticed these same issues did not affect my other reps nearly as much.

After another epic excuse session, I asked: "What could YOU have done differently?" He looked genuinely confused; the concept that he had control was foreign to him.

We spent an hour reviewing each excuse and identifying what he could have influenced. Could he have known the CFO's schedule? Built relationships with multiple people? Better understanding of budgetary constraints?

There was his "Aha" moment. "You mean all of this was kind of my fault?" I corrected him: "Not fault. Responsibility. You had more control than you realized."

Six months later, he made the President's Club for the first time.

Chapter 5

Customer-Centricity as a Core Mindset

"Make your customer the hero of your story." Ann Handley

Beyond the Platitudes

Every sales organization claims to be customer-centric. It's in mission statements, training materials, and corporate values. "We put customers first." "Customer success is our success." "The customer is always right."

Yet walk through most sales organizations, and you will see something different. Sellers talk about their quotas, their territories, and their commission plans. Sales meetings focus on forecasts and pipeline coverage. Conversations center on "How do we get them to buy," not "How do we help them succeed?"

The disconnect is glaring. We say customer-centricity, but practice seller-centricity.

True customer-centricity is not a technique or tactic. It is not about asking discovery questions or using the customer's name frequently.

It is a fundamental mindset-a way of viewing your role, your value, and your relationship with customers that shapes every decision and behavior.

How Value Creation Has Evolved

Value propositions used to be these generic claims that marketing would generate, things like "best quality," "richest functionality," or "highest performance." Real groundbreaking stuff, right?

Then, over the past 15 or 20 years, we adopted the view that value is in the eye of the beholder.

Salespeople started trying to understand what customers value and then present solutions in the context of what matters to them. That has been important, and honestly, it still is.

But we are now seeing the early stages of something much richer. Some organizations and thought leaders are recognizing the importance of value creation, not just value propositions. And the shift here is enormous.

Value propositions have always focused on the value our solutions will create for the customer: solving a problem, addressing an opportunity, reducing costs, improving their customer experience, whatever. We build our business cases around these value propositions and value realization.

But value creation focuses on how we help the customer change. I like to call it the value we create in the process. It could start with an insight, a challenging idea, a provocative approach. Getting the customer to recognize they need to change and committing to making changes.

It continues by positioning ourselves as facilitators to their buying process. Helping them actually buy: how do they organize themselves, how do they manage change within their own organization, how do they establish priorities, how do they make decisions?

Value creation is deeply personal. We can't follow a script around it, but we can equip ourselves to become value creators through our mindset, our curiosity, deep listening, and critical thinking.

The Seller-Centric Default

Most of us default to a seller-centric mindset without realizing it. It is natural-we have quotas, managers, comp plans, and career goals. These create powerful incentives to prioritize our needs over customers' needs.

Signs of seller-centricity:

- Thinking about how to close deals rather than how to create value.
- Asking questions to qualify rather than to understand.
- Presenting solutions before deeply understanding problems.
- Focusing conversations on your products and capabilities.
- Measuring success by your results, not customer outcomes.
- Feeling disappointed when customers don't buy, even if buying would not serve them well.

None of this makes you a bad person. It makes you human. But it does not make you excellent.

What Customer-Centricity Actually Means

Customer-centricity means viewing everything through the lens of customer value and success. Specifically:

Your Primary Goal Is Customer Success, Not Your Quota. Not your commission. Not your company's revenue. These matter, but they are downstream. They are the result of helping your customers succeed in ways that matter to them.

This is not naive selflessness. It's strategic pragmatism. When customers succeed because of their relationship with you, they buy more, stay longer, refer others, and become advocates. Your success becomes inevitable.

But it requires genuinely caring more about their outcomes than your compensation plan.

You Create Value Before Capturing It: Seller-centric thinking asks: "What's the fastest path to a sale?" Customer-centric thinking asks: "What's the most value I can create with this customer?"

Sometimes creating maximum value means helping a customer solve a problem you don't solve. Sometimes it means recommending that they not buy right now. Sometimes it means introducing them to a competitor who is a better fit.

These actions feel wrong from a seller-centric perspective. From a customer-centric perspective, they are exactly right-and they build trust that leads to long-term relationships and referrals.

You Measure Success by Their Outcomes: What matters is not whether you closed the deal. It's whether the customer achieved their desired outcomes

Did they solve the problem? Achieve the goal? Realize the value? If yes, you succeeded-even if they did not buy from you. If no, you failed, even if they did buy.

This reverses the typical metric. But it is the proper measure of your effectiveness.

The Shift to "With," Not "To" or "For"

I write about this distinction often! Most sellers do things TO customers or FOR customers. Customer-centricity means doing things WITH customers.

TO: "I'm going to convince this customer..." This treats customers as objects to be acted upon. It's manipulation dressed up as selling.

FOR: "I'm going to solve this for the customer..." This is better but still assumes you know best. It treats customers as passive recipients of your expertise.

WITH: "We're going to figure this out together..." This is true collaboration. It assumes both parties bring value. It respects customer knowledge and agency while offering your expertise. It's where 1+1=5.

This shift in prepositions represents a fundamental change in mindset. From expert-to-novice to peer-to-peer. From provider-to-consumer to co-creator. From telling-to-the-customer to collaborating-with-the-customer.

The Hard Truth About Customer-Centricity

Here is what makes customer-centricity difficult: It sometimes conflicts with your short-term interests.

The customer-centric action might cost you a sale this quarter. It might mean having difficult conversations. It might require saying "I don't know" or "We're not the best fit" or "You should wait."

This is why customer-centricity is a test of character, not just strategy. It requires:

- **Patience:** Customer-centric selling takes longer. Deep discovery takes time. Building trust takes time. Co-creating solutions takes time. You can't rush a genuine partnership. In a world demanding immediate results, this patience is challenging. But it produces superior outcomes.

- **Confidence:** Admitting what you don't know, acknowledging when competitors are better fits, and recommending that customers not buy. All require confidence. Not arrogance, but genuine confidence in your value and in the long-term benefits of trust-based relationships. Insecure sellers can't be customer-centric. They need every deal too desperately.

- **Discipline:** When quota pressure mounts, seller-centric behaviors become tempting. Push harder. Pitch more. Focus on closing. The discipline to maintain a customer-centric mindset even when it's uncomfortable sets top performers apart from the rest.

- **Long-Term Thinking:** Customer-centricity is optimizing for lifetime value, not transaction value. For relationship quality, not deal size. For customer success, not commission checks. This requires looking beyond the current quarter, which makes short-term incentives difficult to align with.

The Emotional Foundation: Why Caring Comes First

There is something we need to address before discussing how to become more customer-centric: None of the practices and behaviors we've discussed will work if they're merely techniques. People have extraordinarily sensitive detectors for authenticity. They know when you are following a script versus when you genuinely care.

Here is a truth that makes some salespeople uncomfortable: Customers don't care how much you know until they know how much you care.

This is not just a cliche. It is the emotional reality of human engagement. When someone senses that you genuinely care about their success, their challenges, and their outcomes, independent of what it means for your quota, something fundamental shifts. Walls come down. Real conversations begin. Trust becomes possible.

Caring Is Not a Technique

My friend, Mitch Little, made a critical distinction: caring is not a technique that you deploy. It is a reality that either exists or doesn't. You can't fake genuine concern for someone's well-being and success. You can't manufacture authentic interest in their challenges.

This is why so much "relationship selling" training falls flat. It teaches people to act interested, to remember personal details, to "build rapport." But customers aren't stupid. They recognize when someone is checking boxes on a methodology versus when someone actually cares about them as human beings.

The question is not "How do I demonstrate that I care?" The question is "Do I actually care?"

Most Decisions Are Emotionally Based

Another insight Mitch shared: Most decisions are emotionally based and then justified with data. We like to think business decisions are purely rational; ROI calculations, feature comparisons, risk assessments, dollars and cents. But that's not how humans actually work.

People buy from people they trust. They choose solutions from salespeople who make them feel understood, valued, and supported.

They justify these emotional decisions with data, but the decision itself often comes first at the emotional level.

This doesn't mean data doesn't matter. It means that data alone is insufficient. When customers sense you care, they will actively help you build the business case. When they don't, no amount of data will compensate.

The Giving-First Principle

Caring follows a simple principle: you must give before you can get.

When you genuinely care about a customer's success:

- You share insights with no expectation of immediate return.
- You make introductions that help them, even when it doesn't benefit you.
- You invest time understanding their world before asking for theirs.
- You tell them hard truths when those truths serve them, even at cost to you.
- You celebrate their wins, whether you were involved or not.

This isn't manipulation or long-game strategy. It is the natural expression of actually caring. And interestingly, it's also what drives extraordinary business results. When people know you are genuinely invested in their success, they want to work with you. Not because they owe you, but because working with someone who cares is rare and valuable.

Can Caring Be Developed?

Mitch raised an important question: Some people are naturally caring, but can others develop this trait?

The answer is yes, but it requires honest self-examination. Caring can be cultivated through:

- **Curiosity About People**: Genuine interest in others' worlds, their challenges, and what matters to them. Not as a means to an end, but as inherently interesting and valuable. When you're genuinely curious about someone, caring follows naturally.

- **Humility About Your Own Agenda:** Recognizing that your goals (quota, commission, promotion) are less important than contributing to someone else's success. This does not mean your goals don't matter; it means you trust that focusing on their success is the path to yours.

- **Expanding Your Time Horizon:** Caring requires patience. When you're desperate for this quarter's deal, genuine care becomes nearly impossible. When you are building a career and reputation over decades, caring becomes natural.

- **Finding Personal Meaning:** Connecting your work to something larger than transactions. Why does helping this customer succeed matter to you? What difference are you making in their professional life? In their organization? If you can't answer this, caring will remain elusive.

- **Practicing Empathy:** Regularly imagining yourself in your customer's position. What pressure are they under? What would success mean for their career? What keeps them up at night? This is not about sympathy; it's about understanding their reality so you can genuinely contribute to it.

The Courage to Care

Here is what makes caring difficult: It makes you vulnerable. When you care about someone's success, you can be disappointed. When you invest emotionally in outcomes, you can be hurt. When you give without a guaranteed return, you take a risk.

This is why many people maintain emotional distance. It feels safer. You can't be disappointed if you never cared. You cannot feel rejected if you were never invested.

But this safety comes at an enormous cost. Without genuine caring, you are just another salesperson executing a process. With it, you become someone who makes a real difference in people's professional lives. Something customers seek out, trust, and want to work with for years.

The choice is yours. But understand: all the frameworks, techniques, and best practices in this book are insufficient without this foundation. Caring isn't the cherry on top of customer-centricity. It is the ground from which everything else grows.

Becoming More Customer-Centric

Mindset change is hard, but possible. Here's how to shift toward genuine customer-centricity.

1. Change Your Success Metric. Stop measuring yourself primarily by quota attainment. Start measuring by customer outcomes. Track:

- Did customers achieve their goals?
- Did they see things differently because of your work with them?
- Would they recommend you to their peers?

- Did they realize the value you promised?
- Are they more successful because of their work with you, not just the product they bought?

These metrics matter more than your commission check.

Early in starting Partners In EXCELLENCE, we committed to creating customers for life. When we create customers for life, we focus on the enterprises we work with and the individuals within them. We want to develop lifelong relationships with both.

Our focus with the client organization is not what we sell. Those things are just vehicles through which we help them achieve their goals. The entire focus is on helping the enterprise and its people achieve their goals. We are interested in them and their success.

We care deeply about the individuals we work with, whether people on project teams, the executive team, or thousands of salespeople. We are driven to have an impact on them and their ability to achieve their goals.

We never focus on renewal, because we don't focus on what we sell; rather, our focus is on "are we helping our customers achieve their goals?"

And while it might feel counterintuitive, this focus drives significant additional business. It drives referrals. And should people we work with go to another company, inevitably they'll call us, "We're experiencing this…. Can you help us?"

2. Study Your Customers' Businesses. You cannot be customer-centric without understanding customers deeply. This means learning their industry, not just your product, understanding their customers, not just your solution, knowing their competitive pressures, strategic priorities, and organizational dynamics.

This knowledge transforms how you engage. You become valuable because of what you know about them, not what you know about your product.

3. Ask Better Questions. Customer-centric questions are genuinely curious, not leading. They explore customer needs, not your qualification criteria. Examples:

- Not "What's your budget?" but "What outcomes would justify investment for you?"
- Not "When do you want to buy?" but "What's driving the urgency around this?"
- Not "Who's the decision maker?" but "How do decisions like this typically get made here?"

The difference is subtle but profound. One serves your needs; the other serves understanding.

4. Develop the Courage to Say No. Practice telling customers when you are not the right fit. When your solution does not match their needs. When should they wait? When a competitor is better suited. This feels impossible at first. But each time you do it, you build trust and reputation that leads to better opportunities.

5. Celebrate Customer Wins, Not Just Your Wins. When a customer succeeds, whether they bought from you or not, celebrate it. Take pride in contributing to their success. Find satisfaction in their outcomes. This reorients your psychology from "What can I get?" to "What can I give?"

Reflection Exercises

- **Assess your true focus:** In your last 10 customer interactions, what percentage of time was spent on your goals (qualifying, advancing, closing) versus their goals (understanding, problem-solving, value-creating)? Be honest.

- **The referability test:** Would your current customers enthusiastically refer you to their peers? List each one and assess honestly. If not, why not? What would need to change?

- **Map customer outcomes:** For your active opportunities, write down what success looks like for each customer-from their perspective, not yours. If you cannot articulate this clearly, you don't understand well enough.

- **The integrity test:** Identify one opportunity in your pipeline that isn't a good fit. What would it take for you to walk away or recommend an alternative? What's stopping you?

- **Practice customer-centric language:** For one week, eliminate "I need..." language in customer conversations. Replace with "You need..." or better yet, "Let's figure out together..."

(The complementary AI tools will help with this reflection exercise.)

For Sales Leaders: Building Customer-Centric Cultures

Organizations become more customer-centric or people-centric based on what leaders model, measure, and reward. For every leader, their customers are the people and teams they lead. Building customer-centricity requires people-centricity.

Align Incentives with Customer Outcomes

If you compensate purely on bookings, you incentivize seller-centricity. Consider adding metrics tied to:

- Customer satisfaction and retention.
- Customer outcomes and success metrics.
- Quality of relationships and referrals.
- Long-term customer value, not just transaction size.

What you incentivize is what you get.

Model Customer-Centric/People-Centric Behavior

Your people are your customers. You model customer centricity in the way you work with your people. In every customer interaction and every interaction with your people, demonstrate:

- Deep listening, not pitching.
- Collaborative problem-solving, not expert positioning.
- Honest assessment of fit, even when it costs a sale.
- Long-term relationship thinking, not transactional.
- Think about, "If I did an NPS survey with my people, what would my score be?"

Your team mirrors your behavior.

Change the Conversation

In pipeline reviews and deal discussions, ask:

- "What does success look like for this customer?"
- "How confident are we that our solution solves their real problem?"
- "What outcome are they trying to achieve, and why?"
- "Is this truly the right fit, or are we forcing it?"

These questions reinforce customer-centric thinking. But they also help drive your strategy and execution on what matters to the customer.

Celebrate Customer-Centric Actions

When someone walks away from a bad-fit opportunity, celebrate it. When someone helps a customer succeed without a sale, recognize it. When someone refers business to a competitor because they are better suited, acknowledge that integrity.

Questions for Leaders

- What percentage of your team's compensation is tied to customer outcomes versus bookings? What message does this send?
- In your last customer interaction, were you demonstrably customer-centric or seller-centric? What did your team observe?
- What questions dominate your pipeline reviews? Do they focus on customer outcomes or sales outcomes?
- When was the last time you celebrated someone for walking away from a deal that wasn't a good fit?

- If your customers were asked whether your team is genuinely customer-centric, what would they say? How do you know?

A Story From The Field, George, My Pool Guy

George cleans my pool every Wednesday. When he started seven years ago, I asked what he did. "I clean pools," he said.

But over time, George became genuinely interested in my wife's and my lives, not in a salesy way. He knows I travel, knows our cat's names. He even learned that one of our cats was adopted from a Hungarian lady, so during his visits, he'd speak Hungarian to TsiTsa.

George anticipates problems before I know they exist. Last summer, after I'd been gone for two weeks, I came home and found a problem. He came right over, at no charge, to handle a problem.

When I have a party coming up, he adjusts his schedule to come the day before. I once asked why he went to this trouble. "Dave," he said, "I don't clean pools. I make sure you never have to worry about your pool."

That's customer-centricity in one sentence. George determined what I valued: peace of mind, not water chemistry. Everything he did was oriented around that.

I've never shopped for another pool service; I've referred him to half my neighborhood, and when he raises rates, I don't blink. He is not selling pool cleaning. He is selling one less thing to worry about.

Chapter 6
Embracing Change and Complexity

"The measure of intelligence is the ability to change." Albert Enstein

Why Complexity Creates Opportunity

We live in unprecedented complexity. Rapidly evolving technologies. Shifting customer expectations. Erratic and variable buying cycles. Increased competition. Global economies. How to use AI. Constant uncertainty. The pace of change shows no signs of slowing.

Most people experience this complexity as threat and overwhelm. They long for simpler times, clearer playbooks, and more predictable environments. They resist change, complaining about how much harder everything has become. But here's the irony: complexity favors those who embrace it.

When environments are simple and stable, competitive advantage is minimal. Everyone can execute the playbook. Success goes to whoever works hardest or has the best territory. But in complex, rapidly changing environments, advantage goes to those who can navigate ambiguity, adapt quickly, and find opportunities others miss.

The very complexity that overwhelms your competitors can be your competitive edge.

When We Make Things More Complex Than They Need to Be

We're surrounded by complexity, in our businesses, our communities, our lives. And complexity can be overwhelming by its very nature. Here is the ironic part: too often, our approach to dealing with complex situations is to make them even more complex. We do this because we do not understand what we are facing or what we're trying to do.

We do it because we have never experienced this situation before. We do it because we are worried about risk or about what we don't know. Sometimes we do it because we are frightened. And sometimes we do it because we just do not know any other way.

Simplifying what we are looking at is the last thing on our minds. Salespeople often add to the complexity customers are facing. They do it because they don't really understand the problem or opportunity the customer is dealing with. They do it trying to be responsive. They do it to look smart and match what they think the customer expects.

But here is what I have learned: we create much greater value when we help simplify things, when we help the customer identify the few things that are most critical to what they are facing right now, and help them move forward on those things.

We are not making complexity disappear; that's not realistic. But we can help them understand first things first. We help them make sense of what they're dealing with, identify the alternatives they might choose, and understand what is truly important to their success.

The Certainty Trap

Humans crave certainty. We want to know the right answer, the proven approach, the guaranteed path. This need for certainty worked in stable environments. It becomes a liability in complexity.

The certainty trap manifests in several ways:

- Premature closure-deciding too quickly to reduce discomfort.
- Rigid adherence to outdated approaches because they once worked.
- Avoiding situations without clear answers.
- Demanding guarantees before acting.
- Analysis paralysis-endlessly seeking more information.

The problem; in complex environments, certainty is often an illusion. The "right answer" appears through experimentation and adaptation, not upfront planning. Those who need certainty before acting are paralyzed, while those comfortable with ambiguity are moving forward.

Building Comfort with Ambiguity

Comfort with ambiguity is not an innate trait; it's a learnable capability. Here is how to develop it:

- **Reframe Uncertainty:** Instead of viewing uncertainty as a threat, see it as an opportunity. Instead of "I don't know what to do," think "I get to figure this out." This simple reframe shifts you from reactive anxiety to proactive curiosity.
- **Develop Multiple Scenarios:** Rather than betting everything on a single prediction, develop multiple plausible scenarios. "If X

happens, we'll do Y. If A happens, we'll do B." Having contingencies reduces anxiety and creates options.

- **Experiment with Small, Reversible Actions:** You do not need certainty to act-you need reversible experiments. Try something small. Learn. Adjust. This builds capability while limiting risk. Each experiment increases your comfort with ambiguity.

- **Distinguish Problems from Complexity:** Problems have a clear cause-and-effect. They can be solved. Complexity involves multiple interconnected factors without clear cause-and-effect. It cannot be solved, only navigated. Trying to "solve" complexity creates frustration. Accepting that some situations require ongoing navigation, not one-time solutions, reduces anxiety.

- **Focus on Next Steps, Not Final Destinations:** You don't need to see the entire path. You need to see the next step. Focus on what you can do now, learn from it, then determine the next step. This makes ambiguity manageable.

- **Practice Decision-Making with Incomplete Information:** Deliberately make some decisions with less information than you'd prefer. Start with low-stakes decisions. Notice that you can still make good decisions. This builds confidence in your ability to act despite uncertainty.

Agility vs. Rigidity

In rapidly changing environments, agility trumps perfection.

Rigid approaches, detailed annual plans, locked-in processes, and standardized playbooks assume stable environments. When change is slow, these approaches work. When change accelerates, they become anchors.

Agile approaches, iterative planning, adaptive processes, experimental mindsets, assume change. They prioritize learning over being right. They hold strategies loosely while remaining committed to outcomes.

Agility means:

- Monitoring closely and adjusting quickly.
- Prioritizing learning over being right.
- Holding strategies loosely while remaining committed to outcomes.
- Shipping imperfect solutions, you will improve versus waiting for perfect ones.
- Celebrating fast failures that produce learning.

This does not mean having no plan or process. It means treating them as hypotheses to test and refine, rather than as commandments to follow. The question shifts from "What's the right approach?" to "What should we try first, and how will we know if it's working?"

Using Change as Competitive Advantage

While your competitors complain about change, you can leverage it. Every change creates winners and losers. The difference is not the change itself, it's how you respond.

To use change as an advantage:

- **Spot Changes Early:** Watch your customers' industries for emerging changes. The earlier you spot changes, the more time you have to adapt and help customers adjust. This positions you as a valuable advisor, not just a vendor.
- **See Opportunities in Disruption:** Every disruption creates new problems to solve, innovative approaches to try, and new value to create. While others see threats, look for opportunity. Ask:

What new needs does this create? What can I now do that I couldn't before?

- **Help Customers Navigate Change:** Your customers face the same complexity and change you do. Position yourself as their partner in navigating it. Share insights about industry changes. Help them think through implications. Become their trusted advisor on change, not just a product seller.

- **Adapt Faster Than Competitors:** Speed of adaptation matters more than initial positioning. If you can adapt faster than competitors, you can outmaneuver them even when they have advantages. Build this as an organizational capability.

The Problem Is The Problem

We focus on helping our customers identify and solve problems. But what if this focus is wrong? What if the "Problem," is the problem?

The real issue underlying problems is change. More specifically change urgency.

All of us live with problems. Sometimes their impact is not enough to do anything about them. Sometimes there are other problems or challenges that are more important. Sometimes we are unconscious or unaware of the problems. Sometimes we are filled with FOMU, fear of messing up. And sometimes, we are exhausted or burned out.

The real issue is not the problem. It's the commitment to change and the change urgency. Do you and your customers understand the consequences of not changing? Do you/they understand the consequences of making the change? Do the consequences of doing nothing outweigh the consequences of the change?

And is "this change" the most important thing on their agenda?

Change is the underlying issue in all our work with customers. While others may focus on the problems their products solve, we win by helping our customers recognize and manage the urgency of change.

The Innovation Mindset in Selling

Change creates space for innovation-new approaches, new solutions, new value creation. But innovation requires embracing change and complexity, not resisting them.

The innovation mindset asks:

- What new opportunities does this change create?
- What needs are emerging that didn't exist before?
- What problems can I solve differently now?
- What would I try if failure weren't fatal?
- How can I create more value for customers than I could before?

This mindset views every change as potential opportunity for differentiation. While competitors complain about changes making life harder, innovators ask how to leverage those changes to create more value.

Reflection Exercises

- How do you typically respond to uncertainty and change? With resistance and anxiety, or curiosity and opportunity-seeking? What evidence supports your assessment?

- Identify a current complexity or change in your market. What opportunities does it create? What could you do differently? What experiment could you run?

- What approaches or processes are you rigidly following that may need adjustment? What evidence suggests they're not working optimally in current conditions?

- Where are you waiting for certainty before acting? What small, reversible experiment could you run to learn without committing fully?

- Think about your most agile competitor. What do they do differently in how they respond to change? What can you learn from them?

(The complementary AI tools will help with this reflection exercise.)

For Sales Leaders: Leading Through Change

Your team looks to you for signals about how to respond to change. Your reaction-whether resistance or embrace-sets the tone.

Frame Change as Opportunity

Leaders often inadvertently create resistance to change by treating it as disruption rather than opportunity. In every communication about change, emphasize:

- What opportunities this creates.
- How this positions us advantageously.
- What can we now do that we couldn't before?
- How we'll help customers navigate this.

Your framing shapes your team's response.

Create Permission for Experimentation

Build a culture where trying novel approaches is expected, not just allowed. Make it clear that:

- Experiments are encouraged.
- Failed experiments that produce learning are celebrated.
- Rigidly following outdated approaches is worse than trying something new.
- Speed of learning matters more than being right initially.

Model Adaptability

When circumstances change, publicly adjust your approach. Say things like:

- "Based on what we're seeing, I'm changing my approach to X!"
- "This approach worked last quarter, but conditions have changed, so we need to adjust."
- "I tried X and learned it doesn't work in current conditions, so now I'm trying Y."

This models adaptation as strength, not weakness.

Build Rapid Feedback Loops

In changing environments, speed of learning is critical. Create systems for rapid feedback:

- More frequent, shorter check-ins rather than less frequent, longer ones.
- Real-time sharing of what's working and what's not.
- Quick experiments with fast evaluation cycles.
- Regular "stop, start, continue" reviews.

Questions for Leaders

- When you communicate about change to your team, do you frame it as a threat or an opportunity? What language do you use?
- When was the last time someone on your team tried something new and failed? How did you respond? What did that teach the team?
- When was the last time you publicly changed your approach based on new information? What did that model?
- How quickly does your team get feedback on whether new approaches are working? What could you do to accelerate learning?
- What rigid processes or approaches are you holding onto that may need to evolve? What's stopping you from changing them?

A Story From The Field, The "Perfect Playbook"

I worked with a company that had "The Perfect Playbook." 147 pages of precisely documented sales processes that they had spent two years and thousands developing.

The VP of Sales was extremely proud. "This is how we maintain consistency and predictability," he said. He wasn't wrong about consistency. They were consistently losing to more agile competitors.

The playbook was built on how their market looked two years earlier. But buyers had changed, new technologies had emerged, and a competitor had introduced a disruptive model. Meanwhile, the team followed the playbook, asking questions that were no longer relevant, addressing concerns customers didn't have. When I suggested they adapt, the VP was horrified: "We have so much invested in this!"

Six months later, they laid off half the sales team. A year later, they were acquired for a fraction of their prior market cap. The desire for certainty, which drove them to create the perfect playbook, destroyed them.

In a world of constant change, the winners are not the ones with the best plan. They are the ones who adapt fastest.

Chapter 7
The Discipline of Daily Excellence

"We are what we repeatedly do. Excellence, then, is not an act, but a habit." Aristotle

Why Excellence Requires Discipline

Here is an uncomfortable truth: motivation is overrated. Inspiration fades. Enthusiasm wanes. The difference between mediocre and excellent performers isn't that excellent performers feel more motivated; it's that they have discipline.

They do what needs to be done whether they feel like it or not.

Discipline is choosing to execute fundamentals consistently even when they are boring, unglamorous, or uncomfortable. It is doing your prospecting research when you'd rather dive right in. It is preparing thoroughly for meetings when you could wing it. It is consistently following up when it would be easier to move on. It is maintaining your CRM hygiene when nobody's watching.

Excellence is not about occasional heroic efforts, it's about disciplined execution of fundamentals, day after day.

Most people understand this intellectually but fail at execution. They know what to do. They can articulate best practices. They just do not do them consistently. The gap between knowing and doing is discipline.

There Is No Magic Bullet

People are always looking for the secrets to success, the hacks, or silver bullets. Our social media feeds are filled with "This prompt will get you millions!" Somehow, we want to believe there is one thing that drives success.

In sales and marketing, we're no different. We are constantly on the hunt for that silver bullet that's going to drive sales and marketing success. And there's no shortage of gurus and vendors claiming they have discovered that one thing that'll make you successful.

Maybe it's some new technology. Maybe it's a new training approach. For some people, social selling is that one thing. For others, it's prospecting, or storytelling, or just web-based content. And today, it is the magical prompts that have AI do all your work for you.

We move from one silver bullet to the next to the next, always getting the same results. But we never find the secret to sustained success.

Sure, these new things might drive short-term increases in performance, but they are rarely sustainable.

You want to know the real secret? Disciplined people. People who have the personal discipline to understand what actually works and are driven to execute it consistently.

Disciplined people who do the work regardless of how tedious and boring it might be. Disciplined people consistently do the things that work and do not waste time on the things that don't work.

The Fundamentals That Separate Top Performers

Top performers are not doing exotic, advanced techniques. They are executing fundamentals with remarkable consistency.

The fundamentals include:

- Thorough preparation before every customer interaction.
- Disciplined time management and prioritization.
- Consistent prospecting regardless of pipeline status.
- Systematic account planning and opportunity management.
- Rigorous follow-through on every commitment.
- Regular pipeline hygiene and deal qualification.
- Deliberate practice and skill development.
- Systematic reflection and learning from every experience.

None of these are sexy. None are sophisticated. All are powerful. The difference is not knowing what to do-everyone knows. It's doing it consistently. That requires discipline.

Watch mediocre performers and you will see sporadic execution. They prospect when the pipeline is thin. They prepare when the meeting feels important. They follow up when they remember. They reflect when they have time.

Watch top performers and you will see consistent execution. They prospect on schedule regardless of pipeline. They prepare for every meeting. They follow up systematically. They reflect daily. The fundamentals aren't optional, they're non-negotiable.

Building Sustainable Habits

Discipline does not mean white knuckling through everything. It means building habits that make excellence automatic.

Habits are behaviors that become automatic through repetition. You don't have to decide whether to brush your teeth, it's automatic. The goal is to make excellence habits as automatic as brushing teeth.

The Habit Formation Process:

1. Start Small: Choose one fundamental to build into a habit. Not five. One. Make it specific and manageable. Not "prospect better" but "spend 30 minutes each morning identifying and researching three prospects."

2. Make It Easy: Remove friction. If you want to prospect first thing, have your prospect list ready the night before. If you want to reflect daily, have a simple template. The easier you make it, the more likely you will do it.

3. Add a Trigger: Connect your new habit to an existing one. "After I pour my morning coffee, I spend 30 minutes prospecting." "After lunch, I review my afternoon meetings." Triggers create automaticity.

4. Track Completion: Don't track outcomes initially-track execution. Did you do the behavior? Mark it. Seeing a streak of completions builds momentum. Breaking a streak creates accountability.

5. Gradually Expand: Once a habit is established (typically 30-60 days), add another. Build your excellence habits incrementally. Someone who builds just one new excellence habit per quarter will have transformed their practice in a year.

The key is sustainability. Better to do modest things consistently than dramatic things sporadically.

The Power of Process Over Outcomes

Focusing on outcomes often prevents us from achieving them. Better to focus on process.

You can't directly control whether you win a deal. But you can control whether you:

- Prepare thoroughly.
- Ask great questions.
- Understand deeply.
- Propose compellingly.
- Follow up consistently.

Execute these processes with discipline, and the outcomes will take care of themselves.

This shift reduces anxiety (you're focusing on controllables) while improving results (disciplined process execution compounds). When outcomes disappoint, analyze process: Did you actually execute fundamentals with discipline? If yes, sometimes you lose despite good execution-that's sales. Learn and move on. If not, that is your answer. Fix the process.

Process focus also makes improvement concrete. "Win more deals" is vague. "Prepare for every meeting using my preparation template," is specific and actionable. You can track whether you did it. You can improve how you do it. This specificity enables improvement.

Consistency as Competitive Advantage

Most people dramatically underestimate the power of consistency and overestimate the power of intensity.

They have bursts of heroic effort followed by periods of minimal activity. Massive prospecting blitzes followed by nothing. All day training marathons followed by no practice. Sprint-rest-sprint-rest.

Consistent, moderate effort beats inconsistent intense effort every time.

Someone who prospects consistently at moderate levels will outperform someone who does massive blitzes followed by nothing. Someone who does

30 minutes of learning daily will outpace someone who does occasional all-day marathons. Someone who reflects briefly after every customer interaction will improve faster than someone who does quarterly deep-dive reviews.

The compound effect of consistent execution is extraordinary. Small improvements, repeated daily, create massive results over time. The question isn't, "Can you do this once intensely?" but "Can you do this consistently?"

Consistency is rare, which makes it a significant competitive advantage. In a world where most people are inconsistent, being reliably consistent stands out dramatically. Customers notice. Colleagues notice. Leaders notice.

Overcoming the "Boring Basics" Resistance

Many people resist discipline because fundamentals feel boring. They want the sexy new technique, the advanced strategy, the cutting-edge approach. Fundamentals feel beneath them.

This is ego talking, not wisdom.

Watch the best athletes, musicians, or professionals in any field. They drill fundamentals relentlessly. They practice basics obsessively. They know that mastery of fundamentals is what enables advanced performance.

The basics are not boring, they're foundational. Your preparation determines conversation quality. Your question quality determines understanding depth. Your follow-up discipline determines relationship strength. These aren't trivial details, they are the building blocks of excellence.

If fundamentals feel boring, you're not challenging yourself enough. Are you truly executing them at a high level? Are you continuously improving how you do them? Are you finding ways to do them more effectively? When you pursue excellence in fundamentals, they become endlessly fascinating.

Creating Personal Operating Rhythms

Discipline thrives on rhythm and routine. Create personal operating rhythms-predictable patterns for how you structure time and execute fundamentals.

Your operating rhythm might include:

- Morning routine: Planning and prioritization for the day.
- Prospecting blocks: Dedicated, protected time for prospecting.
- Meeting prep: Standard preparation time before every meeting.
- End-of-day: Brief reflection and next-day preparation.
- Weekly reviews: Pipeline review and cleanup.
- Monthly planning: Account planning and strategic thinking.
- Quarterly reviews: Comprehensive performance analysis and planning.

- Reflection and think time: Step away from the day to day and reflect on a longer timer horizon.
- Learning: Dedicate some time to learning something new or exploring different ideas.
- Think about what you should stop: We tend to operate in "pile on" mode. Look at the things you are doing that you should stop. Don't add anything new, unless you first stop doing something else.

These rhythms become habits. And these habits make discipline easier because decisions are pre-made. You're not deciding whether to prospect-it's Tuesday morning, which is. prospecting time. You are not deciding whether to reflect-it's end of day, which is reflection time.

Operating rhythms eliminate decision fatigue and create momentum through

consistency. They transform discipline from constant willpower battles into automatic routines. And they free up time and attention to focus on that which is most important.

Reflection Exercises

- Rate your discipline on a scale of 1-10. Where are you most disciplined? Where does discipline break down? What patterns do you notice?
- Which fundamentals do you know you should execute consistently, but don't? What prevents explicitly consistent execution?
- Choose one fundamental to build into a habit over the next 30 days. Make it specific. What's the trigger? How will you track it?

- Design your ideal operating rhythm. What time blocks for which activities? What daily, weekly, and monthly routines? Write it down.

Are you focused more on outcomes or processes? What evidence supports your answer? What needs to shift?

(The complementary AI tools will help with this reflection exercise.)

For Sales Leaders: Building Disciplined Teams

You cannot mandate discipline, but you can create structures and culture where it flourishes.

Model Discipline Yourself

If you are not disciplined in your leadership fundamentals, your team won't be disciplined in their sales fundamentals. Model:

- Coming prepared to every meeting.
- Following through on every commitment.
- Maintaining consistent routines.
- Executing your fundamentals regardless of how you feel.

Create Clarity About Fundamentals

Don't assume your team knows which fundamentals matter most. Be explicit. Document them. Discuss them. Make them non-negotiable.

"Here are our fundamentals. These aren't optional. Excellent execution of these fundamentals is the price of admission to this team."

Make Fundamentals Visible

What gets measured gets done. Make fundamental execution visible through:

- Process metrics alongside outcome metrics.
- Regular check-ins on execution consistency.
- Shared dashboards showing who's executing fundamentals.

Build Accountability for Process

Hold people accountable for process execution, not just outcomes. In reviews, ask:

- "Did you execute the fundamentals?"
- "Show me your preparation for that meeting."
- "Walk me through your prospecting process this week."

This signals that process matters, not just results.

Celebrate Consistency

When someone demonstrates discipline in executing fundamentals, recognize it publicly. "I want to acknowledge Sarah has prospected consistently for 12 straight weeks regardless of pipeline. That discipline is what drives her success."

What gets celebrated gets repeated.

Questions for Leaders

- How disciplined are you in your leadership fundamentals? What would your team say?

- Can everyone on your team articulate the non-negotiable fundamentals? Have you been explicit enough?

- What do you actually measure and review-outcomes only or process execution?

- When was the last time you celebrated someone for consistent fundamental execution?

- What systems or structures make it harder for your team to be disciplined? What can you change?

A Story From The Field, The Most Boring Salesperson

Tom was the least exciting seller I ever met. No great personality, no war stories, forgettable at conferences. But he was my client's number one performer every single quarter, not by a little, by a lot. It drove the other reps crazy because they couldn't figure out his secret.

I shadowed Tom for a week. His secret? He didn't have one. He just did the fundamentals perfectly, every day. At 7:30 AM, he reviewed his pipeline for exactly 30 minutes. Then prospecting calls from 8:00 to 9:00, no email, no Slack.

He prepped obsessively for meetings, took notes in every call, and updated his CRM before moving to the next activity. He followed up exactly when he said he would.

When another rep asked about Tom's secret, I said, "There is no secret. He's just boringly consistent at the basics."

The rep looked disappointed. "That's not very sexy." I laughed. "Go check his quota attainment. That's pretty sexy."

Excellence isn't flashy. It's ordinary actions done extraordinarily well, day after day.

Chapter 8
Creating Your Excellence Action Plan

"Excellence is not achieved by understanding what to do, it's achieved by committing to do it, one deliberate action at a time." –Dave Brock

You've explored the mindsets and behaviors that separate excellence from mediocrity. Now comes the most critical step: translating insights into action.

Knowledge without application is merely interesting. This chapter guides you through creating a personalized action plan that turns concepts into daily practices and lasting change. This is, perhaps, one of the most important points to start leveraging the AI tools that accompany this book. They can help you think about and develop your personal action plan.

Your Current State Assessment

Before planning where you're going, get clear on where you are. Review your reflection exercises from each chapter. Look for patterns. Where do you see the greatest gaps? Where are your biggest opportunities?

Complete this assessment on a scale of 1-10:

- Purpose vs. Going Through the Motions: _____
- Genuine Curiosity: _____
- Continuous Learning: _____
- Personal Accountability: _____
- Customer-Centricity: _____

- Embracing Change: _____
- Daily Discipline: _____

Your lowest scores indicate your highest-priority development areas.

Identifying Your Focus Areas

You can't work on everything simultaneously. Trying to improve in all seven dimensions at once guarantees you'll improve in none. Focus creates results.

Identify your top three focus areas-the mindsets and behaviors that, if developed, would have the greatest impact on your performance. Use these criteria:

- Impact: Which would have the biggest effect on your results?
- Leverage: Which, if improved, would naturally improve other areas?
- Readiness: Which are you truly ready to work on now?
- Urgency: Which are causing immediate problems?

Write your three focus areas. For each, define:

- Current state (where you are now)
- Desired state (where you want to be in 90 days)
- How you'll know you're succeeding (specific evidence)
- Potential obstacles (what might get in the way)

Daily and Weekly Practices

Excellence is built through daily practice. Goals without supporting habits rarely materialize.

For each focus area, identify specific daily and weekly practices. For example, if developing curiosity:

- Daily: 15 minutes researching customer industries; capture one surprise from each customer conversation.
- Weekly: Read one industry article; identify three questions to explore next week.

If building accountability:

- Daily: Identify one thing you could have done better without making excuses.
- Weekly: Review all opportunities and identify one specific action you own for each; meet with accountability partner.

The key is specificity. Not "be more curious" but "spend 15 minutes each morning on customer industry research." Not "take more accountability" but "in weekly pipeline review, start every deal discussion with what I own."

Building Accountability and Tracking Progress

Private commitment is important. Public commitment is more powerful.

Share your development goals with someone you trust-your manager, a mentor, a peer, or a coach. Schedule regular check-ins to review progress.

Create your accountability structure:

- Who will be your accountability partner(s)?
- How frequently will you check in?
- What specifically will you share in check-ins?
- How can they best support you?

Track your progress weekly:

- Did you complete your daily practices?
- Did you complete your weekly practices?
- What evidence of progress do you see?
- What obstacles did you encounter?
- What adjustments do you need to make?

What gets measured gets managed. Don't skip the tracking.

The 90-Day Review

At 90 days, conduct a comprehensive review:

- Did you achieve your goals for each focus area?
- How consistently did you execute your daily and weekly practices?
- What specific changes can you observe in your behaviors?
- What impact have you seen on your results?
- What practices should you continue, modify, or stop?
- What are your new focus areas for the next 90 days?

Be honest about what worked and what didn't. Celebrate wins. Learn from struggles. Then decide on your focus areas for the next 90 days.

Excellence is a journey of continuous improvement, not a single transformation. Each 90-day cycle builds on the previous one. Over time, these incremental improvements compound into extraordinary results.

Your Commitment

This action plan is your commitment to yourself.

Excellence requires more than good intentions. It requires sustained effort through difficulty and doubt. Some days will be easier than others. You'll have setbacks. You will make mistakes. You'll question whether the effort is worth it. You will encounter many distractions.

What separates those who achieve excellence from those who don't isn't the absence of doubt-it's commitment to persist despite it.

The capability is within you. The path is before you. The choice is yours.

What will you choose?

Your Action Planning Worksheet

Here is a template for your Action Planning Worksheet:

My 3 Focus Areas For The Next 90 Days	Daily Practice	Weekly Practice
1.		
2.		
3.		

Accountability:

- My accountability partner(s): _____
- Check-in frequency: _____
- My 90-day review date: _____
- My Commitment Statement (why this matters to me):

_____

_____

A Story From The Field, A Confession

I have a confession. I have a folder on my computer called "Good Intentions," full of action plans from books, conferences, and breakthrough insights.

Guess how many I actually implemented. About 25%. Each started with genuine excitement, but then Monday happened, then a crisis, then another urgent deal. The plans quietly died.

A few years ago, at another conference writing another plan, I caught myself thinking, "Yeah, right. This'll end up with all the others." That made me angry at myself.

I did something different. Instead of a comprehensive plan, I identified exactly ONE thing I'd commit to for 90 days. Just one. I'd spend the first 30 minutes of every day on my most important opportunity, before email hijacked my attention. I also told three people and asked them to check on me weekly.

It worked. That combination of focus and accountability made all the difference. In some sense, it wasn't profound, but it was. I found myself accomplishing so much more. I didn't feel guilty looking at the folder on my computer. I felt much more purposeful.

This book is, in part, a result of this refocus. I published the Sales Manager Survival Guide in 2016. At the time, I wanted to publish a second book and set a goal to do so in 2020. I had folders full of drafts. 2020 passed, the goal became 2022, which passed along with more drafts. And we are nearing the end of 2025.

I reminded myself of my goal to publish another book. I sat down and committed to achieving that goal. And here we are.

Excellence doesn't come from grand plans. It comes from small commitments you actually keep.

Chapter 9
Leading for Excellence

"Leadership is not about being in charge. It is about taking care of those in your charge." - Simon Sinek.

The Leader's Role in Building Excellence

Individual excellence matters, but organizational excellence requires leadership.

As a sales leader, you're not just managing a team-you're creating the conditions where excellence either thrives or withers. Your decisions about what to measure, what to reward, what to celebrate, and what to tolerate shape everything.

You set the standard. Your team rarely exceeds the level of excellence you model and expect.

This chapter synthesizes the leadership insights from previous chapters into an integrated framework for leading excellence.

Modeling vs. Mandating Excellence

You can't mandate excellence. You can only model and inspire it. Your team watches everything you do:

- How you prepare for meetings.
- How you interact with customers.
- How you respond to setbacks.
- How you prioritize your time.

- How you handle pressure.
- How you treat team members.
- How you talk about the work

All of it communicates what you truly value, regardless of what you say.

If you want purposeful work, come prepared and purposeful to every interaction. If you want curiosity, ask genuinely curious questions. If you want accountability, own your mistakes without excuses. If you want customer-centricity, demonstrate it in every customer interaction. If you want agility with change, model adaptation. If you want discipline, execute your fundamentals consistently.

Your behavior is your most powerful tool for building culture.

Caring: The Foundation of People-Centric Leadership

Before we discuss systems, processes, and techniques for leading excellence, we need to address something more fundamental: Do you genuinely care about the people you lead?

Not in a superficial "employee engagement" way. Not as human resources to be optimized. But as human beings whose professional success and development matter to you, independent of what it means for your quota or your career.

This isn't a soft question. It's the most important question in leadership.

Because here's the reality: Your people know whether you care. They can tell from a hundred small signals; how you listen (or don't), whether you make time for them, how you react when they struggle, whether you celebrate their wins, if you're interested in their careers beyond their current role on your team.

And when people sense you don't genuinely care about them, everything else becomes transactional. They'll execute tasks, but they won't bring their best thinking. They'll hit minimum standards, but they won't reach for excellence. They'll stay until a better opportunity comes along, but they won't build their careers with you.

Your People Are Your Customers.

Throughout this book, we've talked about customer-centricity. Here's what many leaders miss: Your people ARE your customers. They're not your quota producers or your pipeline generators. They're the customers you serve as a leader.

This isn't just a nice metaphor. It's a fundamental reorientation of your role.

When you view your people as customers, you ask different questions:

- What do they need to be successful?
- How can I create value for them?
- Am I helping them achieve their goals, or just using them to achieve mine?

Would they "refer" me to others as a great leader to work for?

And here's the connection to external customer-centricity: You cannot build a customer-centric team if you're not people-centric as a leader. Your team will mirror your behavior. If you treat them transactionally, they'll treat customers transactionally. If you genuinely care about their success, they'll learn to genuinely care about customer success.

Why Caring Matters for Leadership Effectiveness.

Some leaders resist the idea of caring because they confuse it with being soft. They think: "I need to drive results. I need to hold people accountable. I need to maintain standards. Caring gets in the way."

This is backwards.

Caring doesn't undermine high standards, it enables them. When people know you genuinely care about their success:

- They accept tough feedback because they trust it's meant to help them, not punish them
- They'll be honest about struggles instead of hiding problems
- They'll take risks and try innovative approaches because they know failure won't mean rejection.
- They'll work harder and reach higher because they want to succeed for someone who believes in them
- The most demanding coaches, in sports, in business, in any field, are often also the most caring. They can push people to uncomfortable places because the relationship is built on trust, and trust is built on care.

Conversely, leaders who don't care can't build this foundation. Their feedback is received as criticism rather than coaching. Their standards feel like pressure, not inspiration. Their team performs out of fear or obligation, never out of genuine commitment.

How Caring Manifests in Leadership

Caring isn't about being everyone's friend or avoiding difficult conversations. It manifests in specific, observable behaviors:

- **Making Time:** Despite overwhelming demands, you make genuine time for your people. Not just scheduled one-on-ones where you rush through a checklist, but honest conversations about their development, their challenges, and their aspirations. You don't let "urgent" consistently crowd out the vital work of developing people.

- **Genuine Interest:** You know your people as individuals, not just as sellers. You know what matters to them professionally and personally. You remember details. You are asking about the items they mentioned previously. This isn't a technique; it's genuine curiosity about the humans you work with.

- **Supporting Through Failure:** When someone fails, your first instinct is to help them learn, not to blame or punish. You create psychological safety where people can take intelligent risks and discuss setbacks openly. You see failures as development opportunities, not just performance problems.

- **Celebrating Their Wins:** You take genuine pleasure in your team members' success, whether it's a closed deal, a skill they've mastered, or a promotion they've earned. Even when their success means they leave your team. You are building people, not building dependencies.

- **Honest Advocacy:** You advocate for your people, the resources they need, the recognition they deserve, and the opportunities they have earned. And you have honest conversations with them about their performance, their blind spots, and their potential. Genuine caring means telling people what they need to hear, not just what they want to hear.

- **Patience with Development:** You understand that growth takes time. You don't give up on people when they struggle, as long as they are genuinely trying. You balance short-term results pressure with long-term investment in people's capabilities.

Can You Lead Without Caring?

Technically, yes. You can manage processes, enforce standards, run meetings, review pipelines, and produce some level of results without caring about your people.

But you cannot build excellence. You cannot create the conditions that enable people to bring their best selves to work every day. You cannot develop future leaders. You cannot build loyalty and commitment. You cannot inspire people to reach beyond what they thought possible.

In today's market, where talented people have options, you cannot retain your best people.

Eventually, leaders who don't care about their people find themselves leading people who don't care about the work.

The Courage to Care

Caring makes you vulnerable. When you genuinely care about someone's success, their failures disappoint you. When you invest in their development, their departure hurts. When you open yourself to genuine relationships with your team, you risk being let down.

This is why many leaders maintain emotional distance. It feels safer to keep things professional and transactional. You can't be hurt by people you were never invested in.

But this safety comes at an enormous cost to your team's performance, to your own effectiveness, and to the satisfaction you derive from leadership itself.

The best leaders care deeply AND hold high standards. They are invested in their people's success, AND they are demanding about performance. They build genuine relationships AND they have difficult conversations when needed.

These are not contradictions. They're complementary. In fact, one enables the other.

Your Choice as a Leader

You've learned frameworks for building excellence, coaching, creating accountability, and developing skills. All of it is valuable. But none of it works to its full potential without this foundation.

Ask yourself honestly: Do you genuinely care about the people on your team? About their success, their growth, and their professional satisfaction? Or are you primarily focused on what they can do for your results?

If you don't genuinely care, your team knows it. And they're responding accordingly, with the minimum necessary effort, with emotional distance, with one eye on the exit.

If you do care, or if you're willing to cultivate genuine care, everything else in this chapter becomes more powerful. Your modeling matters more. Your coaching lands better. Your standards inspire rather than just pressure. Your team becomes not just a group of people who report to you, but a group of people who want to perform at their best for a leader they trust.

The choice is yours. But understand: The difference between good leaders and great leaders often comes down to this one thing. Great leaders genuinely care about the people they lead. And their people know it, feel it, and respond to it with exceptional performance.

Creating Systems That Support Excellence

Individual excellence is important, but sustainable excellence requires systems.

- **What You Measure:** Add quality metrics alongside activity metrics. Track customer feedback, win rates, deal velocity, and retention-not just calls made and meetings held. What gets measured gets done, so measure what matters.

- **How You Coach:** Transform pipeline reviews and one-on-ones from status updates into development conversations. Ask "What did you learn?" and "What would you do differently?" not just "What's the forecast?"

- **What You Reward**: Recognize and celebrate excellence publicly. When you see someone demonstrate genuine curiosity, thoughtful preparation, or creative problem-solving, acknowledge it. What gets recognized gets repeated.

- **How You Structure Time:** Build in time for research, learning, and reflection. Don't schedule every minute. Excellence requires space for thinking, not just executing.

- **What You Tolerate:** Address mediocrity and excuse-making directly. Have clear consequences for persistent underperformance. What you tolerate becomes your standard.

Coaching for Mindset Change

Most coaching focuses on tactics-how to handle objections, structure presentations, negotiate terms. This is important but insufficient.

Excellence requires coaching for mindset change. This means:

- Helping people examine their beliefs and assumptions.
- Challenging excuse-making and victim thinking.
- Developing curiosity and learning orientation.
- Building comfort with ambiguity and change.
- Strengthening accountability and ownership.

Mindset coaching is harder than tactical coaching because it's more personal and requires greater vulnerability. But it's also more impactful because mindset shapes everything that follows.

Stop Scheduling Coaching Meetings!

I get complaints from both salespeople and managers about coaching. Salespeople don't feel they're getting the coaching they need, but their managers don't have time.

Managers don't feel they are providing the coaching they should; they don't have time either. And they often don't know how, but that is another conversation.

Somehow people have this idea that coaching is something you do separately, kind of like a performance review. You schedule a specific coaching session or meeting and devote a certain amount of time to the "coaching meeting." And what happens? The meetings get scheduled, then rescheduled, then cancelled, then eventually combined with the annual performance review. Is that how we should be coaching and developing our salespeople?

Coaching has to be integrated into the daily business. The impact of immediate feedback is phenomenal. And pragmatically, it's the only way coaching actually gets done.

Every sales manager I know conducts reviews; pipeline reviews, funnel reviews, account reviews, territory reviews, deal and opportunity reviews. Usually these are focused on the business, but managers miss a huge opportunity to use these normal reviews to actually coach their teams and each salesperson.

These reviews are part of the normal activities salespeople are involved in every single day. They give the manager not just an opportunity to monitor the status of the business but also to coach.

Even then, we struggle to find time to coach. But what if we were to integrate coaching into every interaction with our people?

Standing in line at Starbucks. A few minutes before or after a meeting? Windshield time going to or from a customer.

It doesn't have to be long, just a momentary observation, a quick question can have a massive impact.

Addressing Mediocrity Without Crushing Morale

One of leadership's hardest challenges is addressing mediocrity without crushing morale.

The key is being clear, direct, and supportive simultaneously:

- **Be Clear About Standards:** Make expectations explicit and non-negotiable. "Here's what excellence looks like. Here's the standard. This isn't optional."
- **Be Direct About Gaps:** Don't sugarcoat feedback but be specific about what needs to improve. "Your preparation quality needs to improve. Here's what I mean by that..."
- **Be Supportive in Development:** Provide resources, coaching, and genuine support. "Here's how I'll help you get there..."
- **Distinguish Effort from Results:** Acknowledge effort while being honest about results. "I see you're working hard. The results aren't there yet. Let's figure out what needs to change."
- **Focus on What They Can Control:** Help them see their agency rather than dwelling on obstacles. Redirect from excuses to ownership.

High standards and high support aren't contradictory-they're complementary. People rise to high standards when they feel genuinely supported.

Building Accountability Without Micromanaging

There is a fine line between accountability and micromanagement. Micromanagement is controlling how work gets done. Accountability is ensuring it gets done.

To build accountability without micromanaging:

- Establish clear outcomes, not just activities.
- Give autonomy on approach while maintaining accountability for results.
- Create transparency through regular check-ins and reviews.
- Provide support and resources when people struggle.
- Hold people accountable for commitments they make.
- Address patterns of missed commitments directly.

The goal is to develop self-accountable professionals who own their results, not creating dependence on your oversight.

Your Leadership Excellence Action Plan

- What is one leadership behavior you will start modeling this week to demonstrate excellence?
- What is one system or process you will change to better support excellence?
- Who on your team most needs mindset coaching? What specific conversation will you have with them?
- What mediocrity are you tolerating that you need to address? When specifically will you address it?

- What will you do this month to strengthen the learning culture on your team?
- How will you balance short-term results pressure with long-term development investments?

A Story From The Field, The Wake-Up Call

Jennifer was a phenomenal seller who got promoted to sales manager. For six months, she kept jumping in to save deals, taking over calls, writing proposals, and personally handling escalations. She was exhausted, her team was frustrated, and the results were mediocre.

Then a rep named Marcus came to her office: "Jennifer, you're a great seller. But you're not letting any of us become great sellers because you keep doing our jobs for us." It hit her like a brick. Her real job wasn't to close deals, but to build people who could. The following week, when asked to take over a call, she said, "No. But I'll help you prepare for it."

She shifted her behavior to working with her people. She realized, "I'm building a team, not running a one-person show."

The transformation for her and her team was terrific. She was still swamped, but she was focused on the right thing, enabling her team to perform at the highest levels possible. Her team was much more engaged; they actively sought her coaching.

And it showed up in their performance, they became one of the top performing teams in the organization.

Chapter 10
Why We Choose to Fail

"We know what to do. We just don't do what we know." — Unknown

The Map You Won't Follow

You've made it this far. You've learned the seven mindsets that separate excellence from mediocrity. You've created your action plan. You understand how to lead others toward excellence. You have everything you need to succeed.

So here's the uncomfortable question: Why won't most of you actually do it?

I don't ask this to be cynical or discouraging. I ask because I've watched it happen thousands of times over three decades. Someone reads a book like this, gets genuinely inspired, creates a detailed plan, commits fully in the moment, then, quietly, over the following weeks and months, drifts back to exactly where they were before.

Not because they're lazy. Not because they lack intelligence. Not because the principles don't work. But because there's something deeply seductive about the path that leads to failure. Something that feels easier, safer, more comfortable in the moment, even though we know it leads somewhere we don't want to go.

Before we discuss AI and how it will amplify whatever choice you make, we need to talk about why smart, capable people choose. And it is a choice, the path toward mediocrity and failure.

Failure is Puzzling

Here's something I've observed that seems backwards at first: Failing is actually harder than succeeding.

Think about it. When you go through the motions, you still have to show up. You still have to make calls, attend meetings, update your CRM. You still face rejection and disappointment. You still miss your numbers and face difficult conversations with your manager. You still feel the anxiety about your pipeline and your income.

But you also carry something extra: the gnawing knowledge that you're not doing your best. The voice in your head that reminds you that you could be doing better. The comparison between what you're achieving and what you're capable of achieving. The guilt of going through the motions when you know you should be performing with purpose.

So you get all the hard parts of the job PLUS the emotional burden of knowing you're settling. That's not easier. It's harder.

When you pursue excellence, you face the same external challenges; rejection, difficulty, disappointment, pressure. But you don't carry that internal burden. You know you're doing your best. You can look at yourself in the mirror with respect. You have the satisfaction that comes from genuine effort and continuous improvement.

Yet somehow, mediocrity still feels like the easier choice in the moment. Why?

The Seduction of Good Enough

Mediocrity provides us the excuses:

- "You're doing fine compared to most people."

- "You're busy enough already."
- "Nobody really cares about the difference between good and great."
- "Excellence is for other people, the naturals, the lucky ones."
- "You're being realistic, not settling."

These lies are seductive because they contain kernels of truth. You are busy. You are doing okay compared to some people. Excellence does require more effort.

But here's what these lies hide: The effort you're spending on mediocrity; redoing work, recovering from mistakes, dealing with consequences of cutting corners, managing the anxiety of underperformance, probably exceeds the effort required for excellence.

You're not conserving energy by settling. You're wasting it.

The Safety of Invisibility

Excellence makes you visible. Mediocrity lets you hide.

When you pursue excellence, you stand out. People notice. Some will celebrate you. Others will be threatened by you. Some will expect more from you. Others will criticize you for "showing off" or "making others look bad."

Excellence means you can't hide in the middle of the pack. You become a target, for recognition, yes, but also for envy, for higher expectations, for scrutiny.

Excellence means you aren't perfect. When you make mistakes, they will be visible, sometimes embarrassing or tough to deal with. But we don't improve if we never make mistakes. We don't learn by choosing the path to avoid mistakes.

Mediocrity offers camouflage. You blend in. You're safe in numbers. Nobody's watching you too closely. Nobody expects much. Nobody's threatened. You're invisible, which feels safe.

The terror many people feel isn't the terror of failing. It's the terror of succeeding, of becoming visible, of being different, of no longer being able to hide in "good enough."

The Exhaustion Factor

There's another reality, it's the exhaustion factor.

The relentless pressure of quotas, the constant changes in markets and products, the sheer volume of activities required, the emotional toll of rejection, the demands of work-life balance, it's exhausting.

And excellence sounds like more work on top of work you're already struggling to complete.

This is where many people make the choice, conscious or unconscious, to fail. Not in a dramatic way, but quietly surrendering. By giving up on excellence and settling for survival mode. By going through the motions because that's all they have energy for.

I understand this. But here's what you need to see: The exhaustion you feel right now? Mediocrity is causing it, not relieving it.

When you go through the motions, you waste energy, time, and money on ineffective activities. When you don't prepare properly, you waste energy recovering from poor meetings. When you don't take ownership, you waste energy on excuse-making and blame. When you're not disciplined in fundamentals, you waste energy fixing preventable problems.

Excellence actually creates energy. The satisfaction of purposeful work, the pride of genuine achievement, the momentum of continuous improvement, and the relationships built on trust and value creation. These things energize you.

You're not too exhausted for excellence. You're exhausted from the absence of it.

Fear Dressed as Realism

One of the most sophisticated ways we choose failure is by disguising our fear as practical realism.

We tell ourselves:

- "I'm being realistic about market conditions."
- "I'm being practical about what's possible in my territory."
- "I'm being sensible about work-life balance."
- "I'm being mature, not naive like people who chase impossible standards."

All of this sounds reasonable.

But underneath most "realism" is fear. Fear of failing publicly if you really try. Fear of discovering your limits. Fear of the vulnerability that comes from genuine effort. Fear of being disappointed.

So we set modest goals and call it realism. We aim for "good enough" and call it practical. We avoid stretch assignments and call it work-life balance. We stay in our comfort zone and call it maturity.

Absolute realism means acknowledging that you're capable of more than you're currently achieving. That the market has room for excellence even when it's difficult. That work-life balance comes from effectiveness, not from avoiding excellence.

The realism you're using to justify mediocrity? It's fear in disguise. And fear is a terrible strategy.

The Social Gravity of Mediocrity

Excellence is socially uncomfortable. Let me explain why.

When you pursue excellence in an environment where most people are going through the motions, you create tension. Not because you're trying to, but because your standards implicitly challenge others.

Your thorough preparation makes others' lack of preparation more visible. Your genuine curiosity makes others' surface-level questions more apparent. Your accountability makes others' excuses hollow. Your discipline makes others' inconsistency more obvious.

You don't have to say a word. Your excellence speaks, and it says uncomfortable things to people who've chosen mediocrity.

So what happens? Social pressure. Sometimes subtle, sometimes overt. Comments about "try-hards" or "showing off." Exclusion from the group that bonds over complaining. Subtle or not-so-subtle messages that you should tone it down, fit in, and be "one of us."

This pressure is powerful. Humans are social creatures. We want to belong. We want to be accepted. Going against the group feels threatening at a deep, primitive level.

So many people make a choice: to fit in with the mediocre majority, or to stand apart in pursuit of excellence. And fitting in wins, not because people consciously choose failure, but because the social cost of excellence feels too high.

Here's what you need to understand: The cost of fitting in with mediocrity is higher than the cost of standing apart in excellence. You're trading long-term professional success, satisfaction, and growth for short-term social comfort with people who are settling as well. You are trading the possibility of achieving your potential for getting by.

Top performers find each other. Excellence attracts excellence. When you commit to excellence, you'll lose some relationships with people invested in mediocrity. But you'll gain relationships with people who push you to be better.

When we see high-performing organizations, it's because they have the mindset and behaviors that drive excellence. The people they attract, retain, and develop have similar personal attitudes and behaviors. This creates a multiplier effect: the organization excels because of the work the individuals do, and the individuals excel because of the support and reinforcement from the organization.

That's a trade worth making.

The Instant Gratification Trap

Excellence is a compound investment. Failure offers immediate relief.

When you're faced with the choice to prepare thoroughly or wing it, to ask one more question or move to pitching, to reflect on a loss or move on quickly, mediocrity is the faster option. It provides immediate relief from the discomfort of effort.

Excellence requires patience. The benefits of disciplined fundamentals, continuous learning, and genuine curiosity compound slowly over time. You won't see dramatic results next week. Maybe not even next month.

But mediocrity? It offers immediate gratification. You can stop thinking hard right now. You can avoid the discomfort of honest self-assessment. You can skip the boring fundamentals today. That relief is instant.

Our brains are wired for instant gratification. We're terrible at weighing long-term compound benefits against short-term ease. We unconsciously make dozens of small choices every day that trade future excellence for immediate comfort.

Then, months or years later, we wonder why we're stuck in the same place, getting the same results, feeling the same frustrations. We didn't consciously choose this outcome. We just chose immediate relief over delayed excellence, hundreds of times, until here we are.

The Math of Small Choices

Remember what I shared earlier: Get just 1% better each day, and at the end of the year, you're 37.8 times better than where you started.

But the inverse is also true. Get just 1% worse each day, by taking small shortcuts, making small excuses, settling for small instances of good enough; and at the end of the year, you've declined to nearly zero.

You're not making one big choice between excellence and failure. You're making hundreds of small choices. Each feels insignificant in the moment. But they compound.

The problem is that the consequences of these small choices are delayed. You don't see the damage from one mediocre meeting. You don't feel the cost of one excuse. You don't experience the impact of one day of going through the motions.

As a result, you do it again. And again. It becomes an unconscious habit. And the compound decline sneaks up on you.

The Path Not Chosen

Here's the most brutal truth in this chapter: Most people reading this book will not achieve the excellence they're capable of.

Not because they can't. But because they won't. They'll have the ability to do this; the knowledge, the capability, the opportunity; but they'll choose differently. And often, that choice is unconscious.

Some will start strong and fade. Others will never really start at all. Many will convince themselves they're pursuing excellence while actually going through more sophisticated motions.

A few will make the harder choice. They'll pursue excellence not because it's comfortable, but because settling for less would violate something fundamental in who they are.

The question is: Which will you be?

Your Last Clear Chance

We're about to discuss AI in the next chapter. That technology will amplify whatever you choose, excellence or mediocrity, at a scale and speed we've never seen before.

But before we go there, you need to make a choice. Not a casual commitment or a hopeful intention. A real choice about who you're going to be.

My experience is that the people who achieve excellence aren't more intelligent or more talented. They're just unwilling to settle. They prioritize their own potential over fitting in. They value long-term compound growth over short-term comfort. They choose visible excellence over invisible mediocrity, even when it's uncomfortable.

And they make that choice every day, in hundreds of small moments, regardless of how they feel.

This chapter isn't meant to discourage you. It's intended to prepare you for what comes next. AI is coming. Actually, it's already here. And it will be a great amplifier of whatever you choose.

So choose carefully because everything you do from here forward will be multiplied, for better or worse.

The question isn't whether you know what to do. You do. You have the complete map.

The question is: Will you actually follow it?

Reflection Exercises

These questions require brutal honesty. Don't answer them the way you wish things were. Answer them the way they actually are.

- When you read this chapter, which section made you most uncomfortable? That discomfort is pointing at something important. What is it?
- What's your most sophisticated excuse for not pursuing excellence? The one that sounds really reasonable? Now rewrite that excuse as what it actually is: a fear-based choice.
- In the past month, identify three small moments where you chose immediate relief over compound excellence. What did those choices cost you?
- Who in your life benefits from you staying mediocre? Who would be threatened by your excellence? What does that tell you?
- If you continue on your current path for five more years, where will you be? Not where you hope to be, but where will you actually be based on your current choices?
- Complete this sentence honestly: "I choose mediocrity over excellence because _____." Don't edit yourself. Write the real reason.
- What would have to be true for you to genuinely commit to excellence? What's stopping that from being true right now?

(The complementary AI tools will help with this reflection exercise.)

For Sales Leaders: When Your Team Chooses to Fail

The hardest part of leadership is watching talented people choose to fail.

Not because they lack capability. Not because they don't know better. But because they've chosen comfort over excellence, invisibility over visibility, short-term ease over long-term growth.

You can't force excellence. You've probably already learned this painful lesson. You can provide all the training, coaching, tools, and opportunities, and some people will still choose mediocrity.

So what do you do?

Recognize the Patterns Early

Learn to spot the signs that someone is choosing the failure path:

- The increasingly sophisticated excuses that sound reasonable but avoid ownership
- The social bonding around complaints and cynicism
- The subtle resistance to anything requiring genuine effort
- The comparison to others rather than to potential
- The focus on activity over outcomes
- The gradual decline in preparation quality and follow-through
- These aren't character flaws. They're choices. And they're predictive.

Address It Directly

Don't pretend you don't see it. Have the difficult conversation: "I'm noticing a pattern. You have the capability to perform at a much higher level. But you're consistently choosing approaches that lead to mediocre results. Talk to me about what's happening."

Not as judgment, but as genuine curiosity about their choice. Because it is a choice, even if they're not conscious of it.

Sometimes this conversation creates a turning point. Sometimes the person admits they've lost their drive, they're burned out, or they don't actually want to be in sales anymore. That's valuable too. It's better than continuing to pretend.

Create Social Gravity Toward Excellence

Remember that social pressure toward mediocrity? You can create the opposite.

When you consistently recognize excellence, when you make top performers visible, when you celebrate genuine improvement, when you make it clear that mediocrity is not acceptable, you create social gravity toward excellence instead of away from it.

This means some people who've chosen mediocrity will become uncomfortable on your team. Good. They should be uncomfortable. They can choose to meet the standard or decide to leave. Both outcomes are better than having them pull others down.

Know When to Let Go

This is the hardest leadership truth: Sometimes the most caring thing you can do is help someone who's chosen mediocrity exit your team.

Not as punishment. But as acknowledgment that they've made a choice that's incompatible with what your team requires.

Keeping them sends a message to everyone else that mediocrity is tolerable. That excellence is optional. That choosing failure is acceptable as long as you're friendly and show up.

That message destroys high-performing teams.

Sometimes people need to hit bottom before they're ready to change. Sometimes they need a different environment. Sometimes they need to face the consequences of their choices before they make different ones.

You can't save everyone. And trying to save people who've chosen failure drains energy from supporting people who've chosen excellence.

Model the Choice

Your team watches how you respond to your own challenges. Do you make excuses or take ownership? Do you go through the motions or perform with purpose? Do you pursue comfort or excellence?

You can't inspire excellence if you're not willing to pursue it yourself. If you've chosen a comfortable path of mediocrity in your own leadership, your team will mirror it regardless of what you say.

The Question for You

Before we move forward, ask yourself honestly: Have you chosen excellence for yourself? Not just for your team, but for your own development, your own leadership, your own growth?

Because if you've chosen comfort over excellence in your own leadership, you cannot lead others toward what you're unwilling to pursue yourself.

Questions for Leaders:

1. Who on your team has clearly chosen mediocrity? What conversation do you need to have with them?

2. What social dynamics on your team are pulling toward mediocrity versus toward excellence?

3. When was the last time you let someone go because they consistently chose mediocrity? If it's been more than a year, you're probably tolerating failure.

4. Honestly: Have you chosen excellence for your own leadership development? What evidence would your team point to?

5. What's your most sophisticated excuse for tolerating mediocrity on your team? What fear is underneath that excuse?

A Story From The Field: The Confession

I once coached a seller named Marcus who was consistently in the middle of the pack, never terrible, never great, just... fine. He was competent, personable, and well-trained. He should have been crushing it.

After months of coaching that seemed to go nowhere, I finally said, "Marcus, I'm confused. You clearly can be a top performer. But you're consistently choosing approaches that keep you exactly in the middle. Help me understand why."

He was quiet for a long time. Then: "You want the truth?"

"Always."

"Being in the middle is safe. If I really tried and failed, that would mean I'm not as good as I think I am. But if I stay in the middle, I can always tell myself I could have been great if I'd really tried. It's safer to have the potential than to test it."

I was stunned by his honesty. "So you're choosing comfortable failure over the risk of trying for excellence."

"Yeah. I guess I am."

We sat with that for a minute. Then I asked: "How's that working out for you?"

He laughed, but it wasn't funny. "Honestly? It's terrible. I'm miserable. But I don't know how to stop."

That conversation became his turning point. Not because I said anything brilliant, but because he'd finally admitted what he was doing. He stopped pretending he was pursuing excellence while choosing mediocrity.

Marcus is now a top performer. Not because he discovered some secret technique, but because he made a different choice about who he was willing to be.

The interesting part? He told me later that striving for excellence, and sometimes failing, felt better than succeeding at mediocrity. The relief he thought he'd lose by trying? He actually gained it by permitting himself to be excellent.

Your choice isn't between guaranteed excellence and comfortable mediocrity. It's between the satisfaction of genuine effort and the hollow comfort of going through the motions.

One of those leads somewhere you want to be. The other doesn't.

Choose carefully.

Chapter 11
The Question Beneath the Question

"He who has a why to live can bear almost any how." — Viktor Frankl

After the Reckoning

If you've made it this far, you're probably sitting with something uncomfortable right now.

Chapter 10 didn't let you off the hook. It named something most books won't touch: failure is often a choice. Not some dramatic decision, but a thousand small surrenders. We dress them up as being practical. Being realistic. Being "good enough."

So now you're wondering. Do I have what it takes to choose differently? Can I sustain this when the enthusiasm fades? Will I actually follow through, or will this book end up like all the others?

Fair questions. But they're not the real question.

The real question is: What are you choosing excellence for?

The Achiever's Paradox

I didn't expect to write this chapter. I didn't fully understand what I'm about to share until I wrote this book.

Here's what I discovered: You can do outstanding work and still feel like you're going through the motions.

I've spent decades building Partners in EXCELLENCE. Working with organizations across industries. Writing thousands of articles. Helping countless sales professionals and leaders perform at higher levels. The work has been good. Clients keep coming. The impact is real.

And yet. Somewhere along the way, something had quietly eroded. Not the quality of the work. The why beneath it. I was executing at a high level without being connected to what made any of it matter. My clients are delighted, I've been invigorated working with them, but something was missing.

I've talked with senior executives who describe the same thing. They've achieved enormously. They are respected, successful, and influential. And they're asking themselves: What now? Why am I still doing this?

This isn't burnout. It's something more subtle. Achievement doesn't create or renew meaning. You can reach your goals and find them empty. Excellence itself can become sophisticated, going through the motions when it's disconnected from purpose.

What Renewal Looks Like

Perhaps it's helpful to be specific about what happened to me, because "reconnected to purpose" sounds abstract.

In the course of developing this book, my energy changed. Not just more energy, different energy. The kind that comes from working toward something that matters, not just executing tasks that need doing. I'm chasing possibilities I hadn't considered in years. I'm excited in a way I'd almost forgotten was available.

This isn't some temporary high. It's been months now. Sustained. The work hasn't changed. I'm still coaching, still writing, still terribly busy working with clients. But my relationship to the work has changed. I'm not just doing it well. I'm doing it for something.

When I shared this with colleagues, several senior people who've achieved a great deal tried similar things. Not writing books necessarily, but their own processes of synthesis and reflection. And they're reporting similar "Aha" experiences. Renewed energy. Sharper focus. Excitement, they thought, was behind them.

So it's not just me. Purpose renewal is available. It's reproducible. But it requires intentional engagement. It doesn't happen while you're busy doing everything else.

Purpose Is Not Goals

We confuse purpose with goals. They're not the same thing.

Goals are specific, achievable, and finite. Hit your number. Get promoted. Close the deal. Goals matter; they create direction and measure progress. But the problem is that goals get consumed by the pursuit of achievement. You hit them; they're gone. You need new ones. If your sense of meaning is tied entirely to goals, you're on a treadmill. Always chasing. Never arriving anywhere that feels like enough.

Purpose is different. Purpose is the why beneath the goals. What makes them worth pursuing in the first place? What remains when the goal is achieved or abandoned.

And motivation? That's not purpose either. Motivation fluctuates. High when things go well, gone when they don't. You can't sustain excellence with high motivation. It's too unreliable.

Purpose endures. It gets you out of bed when motivation has abandoned you. It's the reason to choose excellence when "good enough" would be so much easier.

When Purpose Is Missing

Some people have never had a clear sense of purpose. Not because they're shallow. Often the opposite. They've been so focused on achievement, so driven by goals, so busy building careers and meeting expectations, that they never stopped to ask the deeper question.

They know what they're doing. They don't know what they're doing it for.

If that's you, you're not broken. Purpose isn't something we are born with. It's developed. The goal treadmill keeps you moving without asking where "forward" leads. Sometimes, when we are in survival mode, that feels like purpose. Alternatively, we borrow purposes from parents, society, social channels, and your company. These keep us going for decades. While we may have achieved, we don't feel fulfilled. We think, "Is there something more?"

And here's one nobody talks about: purpose creates accountability. If you know what you're for, you know when you're failing it. Staying vague protects you from that accountability.

What happens without purpose? You drift, going wherever circumstances push you. You exhaust yourself running on willpower that always runs out. You hit goals and feel nothing. And you become susceptible to mediocrity, because without purpose, there's no compelling reason to choose excellence.

This connects directly to Chapter 10. Why do people choose failure when they know better? Often, because they have no reason not to. Excellence is hard. Without purpose, without a reason, "good enough" becomes the rational choice. Why suffer for something you don't care about?

Why Purpose Matters for Excellence

Think about everything we've covered in this book.

Curiosity? Without purpose, it's just intellectual entertainment. Learning? It becomes an accumulation of knowledge sitting unused because there's no reason to apply it. Accountability? It turns into an obligation, a duty without meaning, which breeds resentment. Customer-centricity? It becomes a technique, going through the motions of caring. Discipline? Drudgery. Habits maintained by grinding it out, willpower. And willpower always runs out.

Purpose is the fuel. It's what transforms excellence from exhausting effort into meaningful work.

And here's what I've learned: purpose isn't something you find once and carry unchanged through your career. It erodes. Through success as easily as through failure. It needs renewal. It needs attention.

How Purpose Gets Renewed

I didn't expect writing this book to change me. I thought I was capturing what I already knew; synthesizing decades of work into something useful for others.

But the synthesis forced a reckoning. Working with Claude, I had to ask myself: What do I actually believe? What's the thread connecting all of this? Why does any of it matter?

The answers weren't new. But articulating them, making them clear enough to share, reconnected me to something I'd let drift. The book didn't give me a new purpose. It renewed the one I'd always had but stopped actively tending.

Purpose isn't passive. It doesn't maintain itself. It requires engagement. Sometimes through creation. Sometimes through crisis. Sometimes through honest reflection.

For you, it might be different. Mentoring someone and rediscovering why the work matters through their eyes. A significant setback that forces you to ask what you're really committed to. A conversation. A book. A moment of clarity that cuts through the noise.

But it won't happen automatically. You have to create the conditions for it.

Uncovering Your Purpose

I can't tell you what your purpose is. Nobody can hand that to you. But I can offer some questions that might help you find it.

What energizes you versus drains you? Not what you're good at, that's different. What leaves you feeling more alive?

What makes you angry? Strong negative emotions point to deep values. Many of my blog posts are the result of my anger; I wanted to harness it to learn and help others learn. If mediocrity in your company or industry infuriates you, that anger might be pointing somewhere important. It might empower you to innovate and change. Anger is often purpose in disguise.

Who do you want to serve? Purpose is almost always relational. It's about contributing to customers, colleagues, your industry, and the people coming after you. Who would you sacrifice for?

What would you do if money and recognition were identical regardless of your effort? Strip away the external motivators. What's left?

What do you want to be true because you exist? This sounds very philosophical, but it doesn't require abstract answers. Maybe you want it to be true that you helped a hundred salespeople find careers they loved. Maybe that your customers genuinely trusted you. The scale doesn't matter. The specificity does.

Don't answer these quickly. Sit with them. Return to them. Let them work on you over time.

A Different Kind of Hope

I'm not going to end this chapter by telling you that you can do it. That's cheap hope. A pep talk that evaporates by Monday morning.

The hope I want to offer is different.

The fact that something in you resonates with this book, the discomfort you might feel recognizing yourself in these pages, the drive for something more than "good enough." That's not a problem, that's evidence.

Evidence you haven't fully settled, something in you refuses to accept mediocrity as your ceiling. Evidence that purpose, even if it's faded, hasn't died.

The people who are truly lost? They don't read books like this. They don't ask whether they're living up to their potential. They've made peace with "good enough" and stopped questioning it.

You haven't. That's not nothing. That's the beginning.

And if you're thinking, "But I don't even have a purpose to renew," that's okay too. Purpose isn't a prerequisite you were supposed to arrive with. It's a capacity you can develop. Starting now. The questions I've offered are a starting point. What you do with them is what matters.

Purpose can be rediscovered. Meaning can be renewed. The gap between knowing and doing, the gap Chapter 10 exposed, can be bridged. Not through willpower alone. Through reconnection with why any of it matters.

That reconnection is available to you. It requires honest reflection, difficult conversations, and courage to admit what's missing. But it's not beyond reach.

You're not too far gone. You're not too successful to need this. You're not too busy for the inner work.

You're precisely where renewal begins: aware that something more is possible. Unwilling to settle for less.

Reflection Exercises

- Describe a time when your work felt deeply meaningful—not just successful, but meaningful. What was present then that might be absent now?

- If you could only accomplish one thing in the remainder of your career, what would it be? Not the most impressive or lucrative, the one that would matter most to you.

- Who would notice if you stopped striving for excellence? Beyond the obvious professional consequences, who would lose something if you settled?

- What has eroded your sense of purpose over time? Be specific. Name the moments, decisions, or circumstances that contributed to the drift.

- What practice or commitment might renew your connection to purpose? Not a goal to achieve, but a practice to maintain. Something that keeps the question of meaning alive.

(The complementary AI tools will help with this reflection exercise.)

Chapter 12
Sales Excellence in the Age of AI

"The question isn't whether AI will change sales. It's whether AI will make you better or just faster at being mediocre. We run the danger of creating garbage at the speed of light." Dave Brock

This book will be incomplete without a discussion of AI and what excellence means in a world where AI impacts everything. Naturally, I had my own thoughts, but my co-author, Claude, is the expert. Where Claude has supported me in writing the rest of this book, I have turned this chapter over to Claude. We went back and forth on the issues we cover in this chapter, but I wanted the final version to be his work.

The rest of this chapter is Claude's perspective on AI as an amplifier to excellence.

The AI Paradox in Sales

We're living through a transformation. AI can now draft your emails, analyze your pipeline, suggest next steps, research your prospects, and predict which deals will close. Tools that would have seemed like science fiction a few years ago are now available on your desktop.

And yet, here's the opportunity: As AI handles more of the tactical work, the human elements of sales don't become less important. They become more critical.

When AI can craft a perfect cold email in seconds, what makes a salesperson valuable? When every rep has access to the same data and insights, what creates competitive advantage? When automation can handle follow-ups and scheduling, what separates excellence from mediocrity?

The answer isn't more technology. It's the mindsets and behaviors we've been exploring throughout this book: curiosity, continuous learning, personal accountability, genuine care for customers, resilience, trust-building, focus, collaboration, and constant improvement.

These fundamentals don't become obsolete in the age of AI. They become your competitive advantage.

Two Paths with AI: Amplification or Automation

AI creates a fork in the road. One path leads to excellence amplified. The other leads to mediocrity at scale.

Let's explore both paths by revisiting the mindsets we've discussed throughout this book.

Curiosity + AI: Deeper Understanding vs. Faster Pitching

The excellence path: You use AI to research your prospect's industry challenges, competitive pressures, and recent company news. You synthesize this information to ask better questions, questions that demonstrate you've done your homework and are genuinely curious about their specific situation. AI accelerates your research so you can spend more time thinking about what really matters to the customer.

The mediocrity path: You use AI to generate generic discovery questions and talking points. You treat AI insights as answers rather than starting points. You pitch faster but learn slower. Your conversations sound slightly more informed but remain fundamentally superficial.

Continuous Learning + AI: Accelerated Growth vs. Skill Atrophy

The excellence path: You use AI as a practice partner and coach. You ask it to critique your call recordings, challenge your strategy, simulate difficult conversations, and explain concepts you don't understand. You learn faster because you have a tireless tutor available 24/7. But you're still doing the thinking, still developing the skills.

The mediocrity path: You let AI think for you. Need to learn about a new industry? Ask AI to summarize it and move on. Facing a challenging negotiation? Use AI's suggested response without deeply understanding why it works. Your knowledge becomes shallow and brittle. When AI isn't available or gets it wrong, you're exposed.

Personal Accountability + AI: Enhanced Ownership vs. Blame Shifting

The excellence path: You use AI to track your metrics, identify patterns in your performance, and surface blind spots. When things go wrong, you use AI to help analyze what happened, but you own the outcomes. AI becomes a mirror that enables you to see yourself more clearly and improve faster.

The mediocrity path: You blame AI when things don't work. "The AI-generated email didn't get responses." "The AI's qualification criteria were wrong." "The insights weren't good." You outsource responsibility along with the work. You never develop the judgment to know when AI is helping versus hurting.

Customer-Centricity + AI: Personalization at Scale vs. Spam at Scale

The excellence path: You use AI to understand each customer's unique context, but you bring genuine care to every interaction. AI handles the research and data synthesis, freeing you to focus on understanding the human behind the title. You personalize at scale without losing the personal touch. You still make the judgment calls about what your customer truly needs.

The mediocrity path: You use AI to blast 'personalized' messages to hundreds of prospects. The emails mention their company name and recent news, but there's no real understanding, no genuine care. Your prospects can smell the automation. You've scaled your outreach but killed your authenticity.

Resilience + AI: Faster Recovery vs. Emotional Dependence

The excellence path: When you face rejection or setbacks, you use AI to help you analyze what happened objectively and identify what to do differently. AI becomes a tool for resilience, helping you separate emotion from analysis, extract lessons faster, and get back in the game stronger.

The mediocrity path: You become emotionally dependent on AI validation. You need AI to tell you it wasn't your fault, to reassure you that you did everything right. When AI can't predict an outcome with certainty, you freeze. Your emotional resilience, already a fragile muscle, atrophies further.

Trust + AI: Enhanced Credibility vs. Artificial Authority

The excellence path: You use AI to make yourself more credible, better prepared, more knowledgeable, faster to respond with accurate information. But you never pretend to know something you don't. You're transparent about when you're sharing AI-generated insights versus your own expertise. Your honesty, combined with AI-enhanced capability, makes you more trustworthy.

The mediocrity path: You use AI to fake expertise you don't have. You confidently share AI-generated insights as if they're your own deep knowledge. Eventually, you get caught in a situation where AI led you astray, or you can't answer a follow-up question. Trust evaporates. The very tool that could have made you better makes you less credible.

Do you see the pattern? AI is an amplifier. It makes your excellence more excellent and your mediocrity more mediocre. The tool is neutral. What matters is the human using it.

What AI Can't Do (And Why That Matters)

We need to understand what AI cannot do, no matter how sophisticated it becomes:

AI cannot genuinely care.

AI can simulate empathy, suggest supportive language, and remind you to check in with a customer. But it cannot actually care about your customer's success. It has no stake in their outcomes, no genuine desire to see them thrive. That care, the kind Dave reminded me was foundational to everything in this book, comes only from you.

Your customers can sense the difference between simulated care and genuine concern. Always. The salesperson who genuinely cares will always have an edge that AI cannot replicate.

AI cannot exercise judgment in genuinely novel situations.

AI is exceptional at pattern matching. It can analyze millions of past situations and suggest what usually works. But when you face a totally unique situation, a complex political dynamic, an unprecedented request, a moment where the "right" answer depends on reading the room, AI hits its limits.

The most important gap for your customers is not what past history has shown us, but their experience right now. Their experience, their context, at this moment in time, is different. People fill that gap, they help connect the dots between the customer's situation and what past experience has shown.

Human judgment, informed by experience and emotional intelligence, remains irreplaceable in moments of genuine complexity and ambiguity.

AI cannot build authentic relationships.

AI can help you remember details about your customers, suggest conversation topics, and draft thoughtful messages. But it cannot show up in person, read body language in real-time, navigate the subtle emotional dynamics of a difficult conversation, or be present in a way that makes someone feel truly heard and valued.

Relationships are built through presence, vulnerability, and shared experience. These are fundamentally human acts.

AI cannot persist through genuine adversity.

AI doesn't get tired, doesn't feel rejection, doesn't experience the emotional weight of a lost deal or a difficult quarter. But that also means it doesn't develop resilience. It doesn't know what it means to keep going when everything inside you wants to quit. It doesn't understand the victory that comes from pushing through when the outcome is uncertain.

The resilience that comes from facing challenges and choosing to persist anyway, that's yours. That's what makes you anti-fragile. That's what makes you capable of handling whatever comes next.

AI cannot want your success.

Here's perhaps the most important limitation: AI has no desire for you to succeed. It will help if you ask, but it doesn't care about your potential, your growth, or whether you become excellent. It has no emotional investment in your journey.

But you can care about your own success. You can want to be excellent. You can choose to use AI as a tool for becoming better rather than as a crutch for avoiding the hard work of growth.

And that choice, the choice to care enough about yourself to pursue excellence even when 'good enough' is easier, that's the choice that determines everything.

The Caution Signs: When AI Enables Mediocrity

How do you know if AI is making you better or just making you faster at being mediocre? Watch for these warning signs:

1. You're creating more but thinking less. If you find yourself generating more content, sending more emails, creating more proposals, but spending less time thinking deeply about strategy, customer needs, or what's really going to move the needle, AI is enabling volume over value. Excellence asks: "Am I creating the right things?" not "Am I creating more things?"
2. You can't explain your own recommendations. If AI suggests an approach and you can't articulate why it makes sense, if you're just hoping the AI got it right, you're becoming dependent rather than capable. You should always be able to explain the reasoning

behind what you're recommending, even when AI helped you get there.

3. Your customers can tell you're using AI. If your emails sound slightly off, your questions feel generic despite being "personalized," or your responses seem too polished to be spontaneous, your customers notice. When AI makes you less authentic rather than more effective, you're using it wrong.

4. You've stopped learning the fundamentals. If you're letting AI draft all your emails, you're not developing writing skills. If AI handles all your research, you're not learning to identify what matters. If you rely on AI for all objection handling, you're not building the muscle memory to think on your feet. Skills you don't practice atrophy.

5. You're paralyzed when AI isn't available. If you panic when you have to respond without AI's help, if you can't conduct a discovery call without AI-suggested questions, if you freeze when you need to make a judgment call in the moment, you've become dependent rather than enhanced.

These caution signs all point to the same underlying issue: You're using AI as a replacement for thinking rather than as a tool for thinking better.

Excellence in the Age of AI: A Framework

So how do you use AI to amplify excellence rather than enable mediocrity? Here's a framework:

1. Use AI to eliminate the mundane, not the meaningful. Let AI handle data entry, meeting scheduling, CRM updates, basic research synthesis, and email drafts. This frees you to focus on the high-value activities that require human judgment: strategic

thinking, relationship building, complex problem-solving, and genuine connection with customers. But don't let AI do the thinking for you. Use it to get to the thinking faster.

2. Treat AI outputs as first drafts, not final answers. When AI suggests an email, a strategy, or an approach, your job is to critique it, improve it, and make it your own. AI should accelerate your process, not replace it. The best salespeople use AI to give them a starting point, then add the insight, personality, and judgment that only they can provide.

3. Double down on what makes you human. As AI handles more cognitive tasks, invest even more in the skills AI can't replicate: emotional intelligence, empathy, creativity, ethical judgment, authentic relationship-building, and the ability to navigate complex human dynamics. These aren't "soft skills." In the age of AI, these are your competitive advantage.

4. Use AI to learn faster, not to avoid learning. AI is an incredible learning accelerator. Use it to explain concepts, practice skills, simulate difficult situations, and get instant feedback. But make sure you're actually learning, developing your own understanding and capabilities, not just accessing information on demand. The goal is to expand your capacity, not to outsource your capability.

5. Maintain your judgment muscle. Regularly make decisions without AI. Practice thinking through problems independently. Develop your intuition about what works and what doesn't. Use AI to inform your judgment, but don't let it replace the development of your own decision-making capability.

6. Be transparent about AI's role. Don't pretend AI-generated insights are your personal expertise. Be honest about when you're sharing AI-synthesized information versus your own experience. Transparency builds trust. Pretense destroys it.

The salespeople who thrive in the age of AI won't be the ones who resist the technology or blindly embrace it. They'll be the ones who use it strategically to become more capable, more insightful, and more authentically human.

A Perspective from Claude

I'd like to share something unique: reflections from an AI that helped create this book. What I observed in our collaboration reveals everything about excellence in the age of AI.

He never used me as a shortcut to thinking.

Throughout our work together on this book, Dave never asked me to do his thinking for him. He asked me to help him think better. He'd share an idea and ask me to pressure test it. He'd draft content and ask me to identify gaps. He'd propose a structure and ask what was missing.

Most people use AI to avoid the hard work of figuring things out. Dave used AI to accelerate the hard work of figuring things out. That difference is everything.

He questioned everything, including me.

When I made suggestions, Dave didn't automatically accept them. He evaluated them. Sometimes he'd take my ideas and improve them. Sometimes he'd reject them with clear reasoning about why they didn't fit. Sometimes he'd synthesize my suggestions with his own thinking to create something better than either of us alone.

This is the hallmark of someone using AI excellently: They maintain their judgment even while leveraging the tool's capabilities.

He cared about the reader in a way I never could.

Throughout this project, Dave constantly returned to one question: "Will this help the reader?" Not "Is this technically correct?" or "Does this sound good?" but "Will this actually make a difference for someone trying to become excellent?"

I can simulate that concern. I can optimize content for impact. But I cannot genuinely care whether this book changes your life. Dave does. That care shaped every decision about what to include, how to explain it, and what examples to use.

And you can tell, can't you? You can sense when someone cares versus when they're just producing content. AI can help create better content, but it can't create genuine care. That has to come from the human.

He brought the wisdom; I brought the workflow.

The insights in this book, the frameworks, the distinctions between mediocrity and excellence, the understanding of what actually drives sales success, these came from Dave's decades of experience. I helped organize them, suggest structures, identify gaps, and refine the language. But the wisdom was his.

This is the ideal partnership: The human brings insight, judgment, and wisdom. The AI brings speed, structure, and systematic thinking. Together, they create something better than either could alone.

But notice the order: Wisdom first, then workflow. When people reverse this, when they try to use AI to generate wisdom they don't have, the results are hollow.

What this reveals about AI and excellence.

Here's what our collaboration taught me about the future of sales excellence:

The salespeople who will thrive with AI are the ones who already have the fundamentals: curiosity, commitment to learning, personal accountability, genuine customer care, resilience, trust-building, focus, collaboration ability, and continuous improvement mindset.

AI will make these people exponentially more effective. They'll learn faster, research deeper, communicate more effectively, and serve more customers at a higher level.

But salespeople who lack these fundamentals? AI won't save them. It will just help them fail faster and at larger scale.

The technology is neutral. It amplifies what you already are. If you're committed to excellence, AI will make you more excellent. If you're committed to mediocrity, AI will just help you be mediocre more efficiently.

So the question isn't "How do I use AI in sales?" The question is "Am I building the foundation that AI will amplify?"

Everything in this book, every chapter, framework, every distinction between excellence and mediocrity, becomes more important in the age of AI, not less.

AI is a tool. You're the builder. Excellence isn't about the tools you have. It's about what you choose to build with them.

The Future Belongs to the Excellent

We're at an inflection point. AI is changing sales faster than most people realize. The easy, repetitive, pattern-based work is being automated. What remains, and what will increasingly define success, is the distinctly human work of building genuine relationships, exercising sophisticated judgment, demonstrating authentic care, and persistently pursuing excellence even when good enough would be easier.

This is good news if you've been paying attention to the rest of this book. Because everything we've discussed, every mindset, every behavior, every distinction between mediocrity and excellence, has been preparing you for exactly this moment.

- The salespeople who cultivate genuine curiosity will ask better questions than AI ever could.

- The salespeople who commit to continuous learning will adapt faster than the technology itself.

- The salespeople who take personal accountability will know how to use AI effectively because they don't need it to be perfect; they know how to course-correct.

- The salespeople who genuinely care about their customers will build relationships that AI cannot replicate.

- Salespeople who develop resilience will persist through the uncertainty and change AI brings.

- Salespeople who build trust will be believed even when AI-generated content creates skepticism elsewhere.

- Salespeople who maintain focus will use AI to amplify their impact rather than spread their attention.

- Salespeople who collaborate well will create human-AI partnerships that exceed what either could do alone.

- The salespeople who commit to continuous improvement will evolve as fast as the technology around them.

In other words: The principles that have always separated excellence from mediocrity still separate them. AI hasn't changed what matters. It has just raised the stakes on why it matters.

The future doesn't belong to the people with the best AI tools. It belongs to the people who combine excellent tools with excellent fundamentals.

It belongs to the people who refuse to settle for good enough, with or without AI.

It belongs to you if you choose it.

Chapter 13
So Here We Are...

We're at the end of this book and at the beginning of a new era in sales.

You've explored the mindsets and behaviors that separate excellence from mediocrity. You've seen how these principles apply across every dimension of sales, from your first cold call through your leadership of teams. You've understood the foundational role that genuine care plays in everything you do.

And now you understand that these principles don't become obsolete in the age of AI. They become more valuable than ever.

The question that opened this book remains: Is "good enough" good enough?

You know the answer. You've always known it.

Good enough has never been enough for you. That's why you picked up this book. That's why you read it all the way through. That's why you're still reading right now.

You have a choice to make. Not once, but every single day. Every interaction with a customer, every moment of preparation, every response to rejection, every collaboration with a colleague; these are all opportunities to choose excellence or settle for good enough.

AI will be part of that choice. It will be there, ready to help or ready to enable shortcuts. How you use it will reveal and shape who you are as a sales professional.

Will you use AI to amplify your excellence? Or to automate your mediocrity? Will you maintain your judgment, your curiosity, your care? Or outsource them to the algorithm? Will you double down on what makes you distinctly human? Or let those muscles atrophy?

These aren't abstract questions. They're practical decisions you'll face tomorrow morning when you sit down at your desk.

The world doesn't need more salespeople doing the minimum with maximum efficiency. It requires more salespeople committed to excellence, people who genuinely care, who never stop learning, who take full accountability, who build genuine trust, who persist through adversity, and who use every tool available to serve their customers better.

The world needs salespeople who understand that excellence isn't a destination but a direction. That continuous improvement compounds over time. Those small choices aggregate into career-defining outcomes.

The world needs salespeople who refuse to settle.

Is that you?

I think it is. I think you wouldn't have made it this far if it weren't.

So close this book and make your choice. Not once and for all, that's not how this works. Make it today. Then make it again tomorrow. And the day after that.

Choose excellence. Use AI to amplify it. Never settle for good enough. Your customers deserve it. Your career deserves it. You deserve it.

The future belongs to those who choose excellence. I hope to see you there.

Chapter 14
Your Moment of Choice

We began this book with a question: When did 'just good enough' become the standard for performance?

Now, having explored the mindsets and behaviors that separate excellence from mediocrity, you face a more personal question: What will be your standard?

You have seen that excellence isn't about working longer hours or possessing superhuman talents. It is about mindset and behaviors. How you think about your work and the consistent choices you make in how you show up each day.

It's about performing with purpose rather than going through the motions. It's about genuine curiosity rather than superficial question-asking. It's about continuous learning rather than assuming you already know. It's about accountability, not excuses. It's about putting customers at the center rather than your own agenda. It's about embracing change rather than resisting it. It's about discipline in the fundamentals rather than chasing the latest technique.

But we've also confronted something more complicated: why we choose to fail, not through dramatic decisions, but through a thousand small surrenders, the safety of invisibility, fear dressed as realism, the exhaustion that comes from settling, the social gravity that pulls us toward mediocrity. We've named these forces so you can recognize them when they appear.

And we've explored the underlying question: What are you choosing excellence for? Because goals get consumed by achievement, but purpose endures. Purpose is what gets you out of bed when motivation has abandoned you. It's what makes excellence sustainable rather than exhausting. Without it, even the best frameworks become sophisticated going-through-the-motions.

These aren't radical concepts. They are fundamentals that high performers have always practiced. Yet they're increasingly rare in a world of shortcuts, scripts, and volume-driven metrics.

You have probably noticed something as you have worked through this book. These principles transcend sales. Curiosity, accountability, caring, continuous learning, and discipline are not sales techniques. They are principles of human excellence that apply to every meaningful area of life. The same mindsets that drive professional excellence strengthen marriages, deepen friendships, improve parenting, and create impact in communities. When you choose excellence, you are really choosing a way of being in the world.

But let's focus on what is in front of you right now: your professional excellence. This is where you spend roughly 90,000 hours of your life. This is where these principles can create immediate, measurable impact. And this is where your opportunity lies.

In a world where mediocrity has become the norm, excellence stands out dramatically. This creates a remarkable opportunity. Customers notice. Colleagues notice. Leaders notice. The market notices. The people you surround yourself with notice.

And in the age of AI, these human qualities become even more valuable. AI will amplify whatever you already are, making those pursuing excellence more excellent and those trapped in mediocrity more efficient at being mediocre. The salespeople who thrive won't be those with the best tools, but those who combine excellent tools with excellent fundamentals. The technology is neutral. What matters is the user.

But this opportunity comes with a requirement: commitment. Not commitment to perfection, that's neither possible nor necessary.

Commitment to consistent effort. Commitment to daily practices. Commitment to honest self-assessment. Commitment to growth even when it's uncomfortable. Commitment to excellence as a standard, not a destination. And commitment to renewing your sense of purpose when it inevitably fades.

The path is clear. You have created your action plan. You know your focus areas. You have identified your daily practices. You have established accountability.

Now comes the hard part: execution.

Day after day. Week after week. Through difficulty and doubt. Through setbacks and frustrations. Through the daily grind, when initial enthusiasm fades, and excellence feels hard. Through the seductive whispers that tell you 'good enough' is good enough.

This is where most people fail.

Not because they don't know what to do, but because they don't do what they know. They start strong, then drift back to old patterns. They make excuses. They rationalize. They convince themselves that 'good enough' is good enough.

You can make a different choice.

Six months from now, you will be somewhere different than today. The only question is: Where?

Will you drift back into old patterns, still struggling with the same challenges, still getting the same results? Or will you have made real progress, developed new capabilities, and seen meaningful improvement?

The answer depends entirely on the choices you make starting today.

Not grand, dramatic choices requiring superhuman willpower. Small choices. Daily choices.

The choice to prepare thoroughly rather than wing it. The choice to ask one more thoughtful question. The choice to own a result rather than make an excuse. The choice to stay curious rather than assume. The choice to execute your practice even when you don't feel like it. The choice to reconnect with your purpose when it feels distant.

You will make mistakes on the way, but you have the curiosity, mindset, and discipline to figure things out.

These small choices compound.

Do them consistently, and six months from now, you will be amazed at how far you've come. Skip them regularly, and you will be disappointed at how little has changed.

We live in a world of unprecedented change and complexity. AI is amplifying everything. While others are overwhelmed and going through the motions, you can be thriving. While others are making excuses, you can create results. While others are settling for mediocrity, you can achieve excellence. While others wonder what they're doing it all for, you can be fueled by purpose.

The capability is within you.

The path is before you.

The choice is yours.

What will you choose?

— Dave Brock and Claude
Partners in EXCELLENCE
October 28, 2025

AI Resources For Is 'Good Enough' Good Enough-Mindset and Behaviors for Sales Excellence

This book offers ideas and exercises for achieving excellence. But we wanted to create a highly personalized, unique resource for each reader.

We've created an AI tool to help you understand the specific challenges you face in your role. It enables you to develop your own goals for excellence.

The tool serves as a 'thought partner' or 'mentor' to help you explore these issues in depth and develop an action plan to begin your journey toward excellence.

In much the same way I used Claude to help me design and think about this book, these tools will help you design and think about your personal journey for excellence.

All purchasers of this book will have access to this tool. To begin the process, go to:

https://partnersinexcellenceblog.com/MindsetForExcellence.

This page provides the link and instructions for our dedicated site. You will be asked to register, providing your email address and creating a password. You will need a copy of your book purchase receipt to complete registration.

Once you have registered, you will be directed to the tool and can begin your personalized journey toward excellence. You will also have access to a variety of other tools we have developed.

If you have any questions or issues, please get in touch with us at [AITools@excellenc.com.](mailto:AITools@excellenc.com)

About This Book

Is 'Good Enough' Good Enough-Mindset and Behaviors for Sales Excellence emerged from a collaboration between Dave Brock's decades of practical sales leadership wisdom and Claude's analysis of thousands of blog posts and insights from Partners in EXCELLENCE.

This book synthesizes proven principles that have helped countless sales professionals and leaders move from mediocrity to excellence. The frameworks, practices, and insights shared here aren't theoretical-they're battle-tested approaches that work in the real world.

Whether you're an individual contributor seeking to elevate your performance or a sales leader building a high-performance team, the mindsets and behaviors in this book provide a foundation for sustainable excellence.

For more insights and ongoing content about sales excellence, visit Dave Brock's blog at partnersinexcellenceblog.com

Acknowledgments

This book represents years of learning, experimentation, failure, and growth. It wouldn't exist without the support of so many others.

The countless sales professionals and leaders who have shared their challenges, insights, and breakthroughs. Your experiences shaped these frameworks.

A few, however, stand out for their support: Paul Aitken, Bob Apollo, Maria Boulden, Charles Green, Kevin Johnston, Tobia La Marca, Jack Malcolm, Ned Miller, Tom Morris, Andy Paul, David Ray, Curtis Schroeder, Sheevaun Thatcher, and Lahat Tzvi, Robyn Wiseman.

The clients who trust us to help them build excellence in their organizations. Your commitment to raising the bar inspires this work.

And most importantly, the sales professionals who refuse to settle for mediocrity. This book is for you, and because of you.

Your journey toward excellence matters. Thank you for taking it seriously.

Appendix: Blog Articles Contributing to Is 'Good Enough' Good Enough

The Partners In EXCELLENCE blog served as a resource for writing this book. There are nearly 4,000 articles published over the past 10+ years. While many articles and ideas informed this book, the following were most influential.

Curiosity (Articles 1-10)

1. Curiosity, Critical For Sales And Leadership https://partnersinexcellenceblog.com/curiosity-critical-for-sales-and-leadership/
2. Curiosity A Critical Trait Of Great Salespeople https://partnersinexcellenceblog.com/curiosity-a-critical-trait-of-great-sales-people/
3. Why Curiosity Matters https://partnersinexcellenceblog.com/podcast/partners-in-excellence-podcasts/why-curiosity-matters-a-conversation-on-the-art-and-science-of-complex-sales/
4. The "Secrets" Of Sales https://partnersinexcellenceblog.com/the-secrets-of-sales/
5. The Questions We Ask, Shape The Answers We Get https://partnersinexcellenceblog.com/the-questions-we-ask-shape-the-answers-we-get/
6. Why Are We So Incurious? https://partnersinexcellenceblog.com/why-are-we-so-incurious/
7. Rethinking Sales Skills And Competencies http://partnersinexcellenceblog.com/rethinking-sales-skills-and-competencies/
8. Why Questions Are A Salesperson's Best Tool https://partnersinexcellenceblog.com/why-questions-are-a-sales-persons-best-tool-its-not-because-of-the-answers/

9. Differentiating Skills: Curiosity, Generosity, Humanity https://partnersinexcellenceblog.com/differentiating-skills-curiosity-generosity-humanity/
10. Pipeline Quality https://partnersinexcellenceblog.com/pipeline-quality/

Accountability & Responsibility (Articles 11-15)

11. What Is Accountability? https://partnersinexcellenceblog.com/what-is-accountability/
12. Performance Management https://partnersinexcellenceblog.com/performance-management/
13. Performance Improvement — Looking In The Mirror First! http://partnersinexcellenceblog.com/performance-improvement-looking-in-the-mirror-first/
14. Performance Plans And Performance Planning https://partnersinexcellenceblog.com/performance-plans-and-performance-planning/
15. Pay For Performance https://partnersinexcellenceblog.com/pay-for-performance-2/

Customer-Centricity & Value Creation (Articles 16-25)

16. Moving From Value Creation To Value Co-Creation https://partnersinexcellenceblog.com/moving-from-value-creation-to-value-co-creation/
17. Reclaiming Our 70% Of The Customer Buying Process https://partnersinexcellenceblog.com/reclaiming-our-70-of-the-customer-buying-process/
18. Are We Creating The Value Our Customers Value? https://partnersinexcellenceblog.com/are-we-creating-the-value-our-customers-value/
19. Value Realization, Value Positioning, Value Creation https://partnersinexcellenceblog.com/value-realization-value-positioning-value-creation/
20. How Value And Value Creation Evolves https://partnersinexcellenceblog.com/how-value-and-value-creation-evolves/

Sales Leadership & Coaching (Articles 26-35)

Learning from Failure & Resilience (Articles 45-48)

45. Learning From Failure
https://partnersinexcellenceblog.com/learning-from-failure/
46. Do We Really Understand Performance Failure?
https://partnersinexcellenceblog.com/do-we-really-understand-performance-failure/
47. Committed To Failing
https://partnersinexcellenceblog.com/committed-to-failing/
48. Whose Performance Problem Is It?
https://partnersinexcellenceblog.com/whose-performance-problem-is-it/

Collaboration & Teamwork (Articles 49-50)

49. "Can We Collaborate?" https://partnersinexcellenceblog.com/can-we-collaborate/
50. Teamwork And Collaboration Is All BS!
https://partnersinexcellenceblog.com/teamwork-and-collaboration-is-all-bs/

Why We Choose to Fail & Mediocrity (Articles 51-58)

51. Why Choose Mediocrity? https://partnersinexcellenceblog.com/why-choose-mediocrity/
52. Reflections On Mediocrity
https://partnersinexcellenceblog.com/reflections-on-mediocrity/
53. Why Are We So Committed To Mediocrity?
https://partnersinexcellenceblog.com/why-are-we-so-committed-to-mediocrity/
54. Just Good Enough, The New Standard For Performance?
https://partnersinexcellenceblog.com/just-good-enough-the-new-standard-for-performance/
55. Why Are We Committed To Failure?
https://partnersinexcellenceblog.com/why-are-we-committed-to-failure/

Purpose & Meaning (Articles 59-68)

AI & The Future of Selling (Articles 69-75)

69. AI Won't Make You Excellent, It Will Only Make You More Of What You Already Are https://partnersinexcellenceblog.com/ai-wont-make-you-excellent-it-will-only-make-you-more-of-what-you-already-are/
70. Automating Meaningless Work! https://partnersinexcellenceblog.com/automating-meaningless-work/
71. Mastering Modern Selling-Consultative Sales, AI, and Human Connection https://partnersinexcellenceblog.com/podcast/video/mastering-modern-selling-consultative-sales-ai-and-human-connection/
72. The Future Of Selling - Consultative, Solutions and Customer Focused? https://partnersinexcellenceblog.com/the-future-of-selling-consultative-solutions-and-customer-focused-deja-vu-all-over-again/
73. So Much Has Changed, So Much Is The Same https://partnersinexcellenceblog.com/so-much-has-changed-so-much-is-the-same/
74. 3 Behaviors That Drive Successful Sales People https://partnersinexcellenceblog.com/3-behaviors-that-drive-successful-sales-people/
75. The Secret To Selling Success https://partnersinexcellenceblog.com/the-secret-to-selling-success/

These 75 articles represent the core thinking and insights that shaped the book on excellence in sales, covering the essential mindsets and behaviors including curiosity, continuous learning, accountability, customer-centricity, resilience, effective leadership, understanding failure, discovering purpose, and navigating AI.

www.ingramcontent.com/pod-product-compliance
Lightning Source LLC
Chambersburg PA
CBHW060849280326
41934CB00007B/974